RELATIONAL INTELLIGENCE

The Key Factor to Exceptional
School Leadership

Dr. Brad Johnson &
Dr. Rachel Edoho-Eket

Relational Intelligence

Published by TeacherGoals Publishing, LLC, Beech Grove, IN
www.teachergoals.com
Cover Design by: Tricia Fuglestad
Interior Design by: Zoe Howard
Edited by: Dr. John Wick, Ed.D.

Library of Congress Control Number: 2025940472
Paperback ISBN: 978-1-959419-33-4
ASIN: B0FCYXYK2L

First Printing July 2025

PRAISE FOR *RELATIONAL INTELLIGENCE*

Brad Johnson and Rachel Edoho-Eket are absolutely right to put *Relational Intelligence* at the center of school administration. Public education is a people business. You can have all the PhDs in the world, but if they aren't working together, good luck getting anything done. They have the right diagnosis for what ails so many school districts, and their book is the cure.

 ~ *Dr. Stephanie S. Elizalde Superintendent of Dallas ISD*

In their compelling new book, Dr. Brad Johnson and Dr. Rachel Edoho-Eket illuminate the essential role of relational intelligence (RQ) in effective educational leadership. Through rich storytelling and actionable insights, they show how authenticity, trust, and meaningful connection empower school leaders to build strong communities and lasting impact. This is a must-read for any educator committed to leading with heart and purpose.

 ~ *Dr. Jen Schwanke, author, keynote speaker, and district administrator*

Relational Intelligence by Dr. Brad Johnson and Dr. Rachel Edoho-Eket is a powerful reminder that leadership is rooted in the strength of relationships. This book shows how trust, communication, and genuine connection are the keys to inspiring and empowering teams. It's an essential read for anyone wanting to lead with heart and create lasting impact.

 ~ *Zac Bauermaster, principal, speaker, and author of* Leading with a Humble Heart and Leading with People

In *Relational Intelligence: The Key Factor to Exceptional School Leadership*, you will discover the power of relationships, trust, vulnerability, and connection. What I love most about this book is its practicality. The stories are rich and heartfelt, and the applications are shared in ways you can apply to any setting. If you want to learn school leadership, lean into the experiences of Dr. Rachel Edoho-Eket and Dr. Brad Johnson.

 ~ *William D. Parker, Founder, Principal Matters, LLC*

DEDICATION

To the passionate leaders who give their hearts to the work of education—this book is for you. Each day, you step into your schools as leaders and visionaries, mentors, and champions for the students, teachers, and families you serve. Protocols and programs do not measure your leadership, but by the lives you touch and the hope you inspire.

Thank you for your commitment and for leading with love, even when the path is challenging. The work you do matters—more than you may ever know. May this book remind you that authentic leadership is an act of service and that the impact of your kindness, courage, and compassion will ripple far beyond what you will ever see. Keep leading with your heart, and never lose sight of the incredible difference you are making.

With gratitude,

Dr. Rachel Edoho-Eket

To all the educational leaders who dedicate themselves tirelessly to creating supportive, empowering environments—thank you. Your unwavering commitment to the growth and success of your teachers shapes not only classrooms but entire communities. You inspire, uplift, and lead by example, making a lasting impact on the lives of both students and educators. This book is for you—may it fuel your passion and remind you of the profound difference you make every day.

Thank you!

Dr. Brad Johnson

CONTENTS

INTRODUCTION

Imagine walking into your school each morning, greeted by a team that's not just going through the motions, but truly energized, aligned with your vision, and ready to tackle any challenge that comes their way. The atmosphere is electric, collaboration is second nature, and every staff member feels supported, valued, and motivated. This isn't a distant dream; this is the power of prioritizing relationships in leadership.

As a teacher, administrator, and college professor, I've witnessed the profound impact relationships can have on school culture, teacher effectiveness, and ultimately, student achievement. That's why Relational Intelligence (RQ) has become the cornerstone of my work.

Relational Intelligence (RQ), a term coined by Dr. Tony Bandelli (2013), is similar to IQ (Intelligence Quotient) or EQ (Emotional Intelligence), but with a specific focus on how well we understand, manage, and utilize relationships in all areas of life. Dr. Bandelli defines RQ as "the ability to understand and manage relationships effectively to create environments where people can work together productively and with trust." While IQ measures cognitive ability and EQ assesses emotional awareness and regulation, RQ centers on our ability to connect with others, foster trust, and build collaborative environments that drive success. RQ isn't just a skill—it's the skill that makes leadership possible.

After 30 years in education, traveling the world, speaking with top leaders, and mentoring others, one truth stands clear: Relational Intelligence is the key to exceptional leadership.

When leaders foster trust, collaboration, and a shared sense of purpose, it leads to stronger teacher morale and greater job satisfaction.

When it comes to leadership, relationships are more than just a nice-to-have. They are the foundation of everything you do. Research backs this up in a big way. According to John Hattie's meta-analysis (2009), the relationship between administrators and teachers plays a crucial role in improving learning outcomes. Strong leadership can powerfully affect teacher motivation, instructional quality, and retention, directly impacting student success.

And it doesn't stop there. Leithwood & Jantzi's (2006) research on transformational leadership highlights that when leaders foster trust, collaboration, and a shared sense of purpose, it leads to stronger teacher morale and greater job satisfaction. This, in turn, makes teachers more effective, which ultimately boosts student performance.

Further research from The New Teacher Center (2016) reinforces the idea that principal leadership directly influences teacher effectiveness and retention. In schools with strong, supportive principals, teachers are more likely to stay in the profession and perform at a higher level, leading to more stable, high-performing schools.

I'm fortunate to collaborate with a leader who shares my passion for relational intelligence in leadership. As a principal and mentor, she has seen firsthand how powerful building strong, authentic relationships can be in transforming a school. We wanted to combine our expertise and vision to create a resource that empowers leaders to prioritize relationships and foster the kind of school culture that supports personal and professional growth—working alongside someone who values relational intelligence as profoundly as I do has been inspiring and validating—proof that we can create the best possible school environments when we focus on building the best relationships.

In this book, we will show you how to develop and refine your Relational Intelligence, transforming not only your relationships with your team but also the very culture of your school. When you lead with relational intelligence, everyone in your school—students, teachers, and leaders alike—excels.

PILLAR ONE:
Trust – The Foundation of Exceptional Leadership

Let's be honest—most people don't step into leadership because they're natural-born leaders. They get promoted because they were rockstars at their previous job. Maybe they were an incredible teacher, a data guru, or someone who could keep the wheels from falling off.

But here's the problem: being great at a job and being great at leading people are two completely different skill sets.

Leadership isn't about what you can accomplish but how well you can bring others along with you. And if you don't master Relational Intelligence, you're in for a rough ride.

Before you start thinking, "Great, another buzzword to add to the list," let me stop you right there.

RQ is not about being outgoing, extroverted, or naturally charismatic. It's not a personality trait or just another "soft skill." Relational Intelligence is the ability to connect with others on a deeper level, to build trust, communicate effectively, and create genuine relationships that empower and inspire. It's the most critical leadership skill because you'll struggle to lead effectively without it.

> Leaders with strong Relational Intelligence build more than just teams— they create environments where people thrive.

Relational Intelligence isn't something you're born with; it's something you can develop—whether you're an introvert, extrovert, or anywhere in between. Mastering RQ isn't about becoming someone you're not. It's about cultivating the skills necessary to build meaningful connections that enhance your leadership, no matter your personality type.

I define Relational Intelligence as the ability to build strong, trusting, and meaningful relationships through communication, emotional awareness, and the understanding that leadership is fundamentally about people. It goes beyond soft skills and develops intentionally to create collaborative teams, communicate openly, and stay committed to the shared vision. In essence, it's the key to unlocking the potential of any team, and without it, leadership falls apart.

So why should you care about cultivating high RQ in your leadership? Because the benefits are far-reaching and impactful. Leaders with strong Relational Intelligence build more than just teams—they create environments where people thrive. Here are a few of the most powerful outcomes of a leader with strong Relational Intelligence:

- **More Engaged Staff**: Leaders who connect with their team members on a deeper level see higher levels of engagement. When employees feel valued, they are more likely to contribute ideas, take initiative, and put in extra effort to see projects succeed. This engagement leads to a more productive, creative, and innovative team (Kouzes & Posner, 2017).
- **Lower Turnover**: People don't quit jobs—they quit leaders. When leadership is rooted in relational intelligence, employees stay because they trust their leaders and feel appreciated. High relational intelligence (RQ) fosters a culture of stability, where people want to stay and grow with the team, ultimately reducing turnover and retaining top talent (Goleman, 2013).
- **Higher Job Satisfaction**: When staff feel recognized, valued, and supported by their leader, job satisfaction soars. High RQ leadership creates an environment where individuals are motivated to give their best, leading to greater fulfillment in their work. This translates into better morale, a positive workplace atmosphere, and improved outcomes for the organization (McKee, Boyatzis, & Johnston, 2008).
- **Stronger Team Collaboration**: Great leaders with high RQ know how to foster a culture of collaboration. By building trust and encouraging open communication. The result is a team that solves problems effectively, shares innovative ideas, and produces high-quality work (Lencioni, 2012).
- **Resilience During Challenges**: Leadership isn't just about shining in the good times—it's about guiding your team through difficult moments. Leaders with strong RQ create a sense of safety and support, making it easier for teams to navigate challenges and bounce back stronger. This resilience leads to quicker recovery from setbacks and a more adaptable team (Avolio & Gardner, 2005).

By developing relational intelligence, you're not just improving your leadership effectiveness; you're creating a team that is engaged, loyal, and ready to tackle any challenge together. The benefits of high RQ go beyond just improving your leadership skills—they transform your entire organization into a more connected, motivated, and successful team.

The 3 Pillars of RQ That Lead to Exceptional Leadership

In this book, we'll focus on the three pillars of Relational Intelligence that, when developed, lead to exceptional leadership:

1. **Trust** – The foundation of every strong team. Trust is built through consistency, integrity, and follow-through. Without it, leadership collapses.
2. **Communication** – It's not just about talking, it's about ensuring that people truly understand, feel heard, and stay aligned with the vision. Good communication flows in both directions.
3. **Connection** – The ability to forge real, lasting bonds with your team. Connection isn't about being liked or popular; it's about creating a sense of unity, commitment, and shared purpose.

These three pillars are the keys to becoming an exceptional leader. With strong Relational Intelligence, your leadership will be defined by your ability to inspire and engage your team, not by your title or position. Leadership isn't about control or command—it's about creating a space where trust, communication, and connection can thrive.

So, let's start with the first pillar: Trust.

Trust: The Leadership Game-Changer

Think of the best leader you've ever worked with. Oddly, you didn't follow them because of their job title but because you trusted them.

Without trust, nothing else works. Communication falls flat. Collaboration disappears. Your team stops taking risks, stops sharing ideas, and starts doing just enough to get by. And if you think trust is just a "nice-to-have," let's talk about what happens when it's missing.

According to Gallup (2017), 50% of employees, including teachers, who quit their jobs do so because of their boss. That's not just a statistic—that's an epidemic.

Trust is the glue that holds everything together. And here's the kicker: it's not just about whether people trust you to do the job. It's about whether they trust that you have their backs, that you lead with integrity, and that when things get tough, you won't throw them under the bus.

Building Trust: What It Takes

Trust isn't something given; it's something earned. And no, you can't fake it with an open-door policy and a few team-building activities. It's built through small, consistent actions that prove to your team that you're reliable, transparent, and invested in their success.

Most leaders get it wrong when they assume trust comes from words. It doesn't. It comes from actions.

- Show up. Be present. Be available. Be engaged.
- Follow through. Nothing erodes trust faster than a leader who makes promises they never keep.
- Be honest. People don't need a perfect leader—they need an honest one. Own your mistakes, and don't pretend to have all the answers.
- Listen more than you speak. Trust isn't about being the loudest voice in the room. It's about making people feel heard.

And here's the best part: Everything else becomes more manageable when trust is strong. Communication flows naturally. Connection becomes effortless. And your team? They'll go all in—because they know you've got their back.

What's Next?

Trust is just the beginning. The following two pillars—Communication and Connection—are just as crucial. But without trust, they simply can not exist, at least not effectively.

In this first section, we're diving deep into trust—how to build, strengthen, and repair it if it's broken or doesn't exist.

Because at the end of the day, leadership isn't about control—it's about trust. And when you get trust right, the rest of leadership starts to fall into place.

Let's get started.

CHAPTER ONE
The Secret Sauce: How Relational Intelligence Transforms Leadership

The Secret Sauce: Are You a Chef or Just a Cook?

Think about the best leader you've ever worked with. What made them stand out? Was it their knowledge? Their ability to make tough decisions? Or was it something more challenging to define—the way they made you feel valued, heard, and motivated to give your best?

Now, think about a leader who struggled. Maybe they had the credentials, the title, or the experience, but something was missing. People followed because they had to, not because they wanted to. The difference? It all comes down to RQ—Relational Intelligence.

Outstanding leadership isn't just about what you do but how you do it.

Let's break it down with a familiar analogy. Imagine walking into a busy kitchen. Someone carefully follows a recipe on one side—measuring each ingredient and double-checking the instructions. That's the cook. On the other hand, someone moves with rhythm and intuition. They add a pinch of this, a splash of that, adjusting as they go. That's the chef.

The cook delivers a fine meal, technically correct and good. But the chef creates something memorable with flavor, creativity, and personality. Leadership works the same way.

Many leaders follow strategies, checklists, and protocols like a cook follows a recipe. And while that might get the job done, it rarely inspires. Exceptional leaders are more like chefs. They blend strategy with empathy, timing with emotional awareness, and they know how to read the room like a seasoned chef reads the heat of a pan.

Like every great chef has a *secret sauce*, great leaders do. That secret sauce is **Relational Intelligence**.

Leadership without relational intelligence is like a meal without seasoning—technically complete but lacking soul. But when you add that secret sauce, everything changes. Morale rises. Teams excel. Trust deepens. And the impact of your leadership becomes something people talk about long after the moment has passed.

Relational intelligence isn't a soft skill—it's a *signature skill*. It's what separates average leaders from transformational ones. It's the key ingredient that turns a role of authority into a force of influence.

This chapter will examine how to tap into that chef-like, adaptive leadership style. Trust me—it will turn everyday challenges into opportunities for connection and growth. So, grab your apron. Let's start cooking up some leadership magic, one conversation at a time.

The 3 Key Ingredients of RQ Leadership (The Secret Sauce)

As discussed in the introduction, the foundation of Relational Intelligence leadership is built on three essential pillars. These key ingredients distinguish between a leader who simply manages and one who truly inspires and empowers their team. Let's take a closer look at these three core principles:

Connection Over Compliance

Imagine walking into a room where people light up the moment you enter. They don't just clock in; they're excited to be there because they feel seen and valued. That's the magic of Connection Over Compliance. It's not about enforcing rules from above but building relationships based on respect, trust, and authenticity.

Think about a time you worked for someone who treated you like another machine cog. Now, think about the leader who took the time to understand you, your challenges, goals, and dreams. Which one would you follow with more enthusiasm? Investing in your team creates a culture where everyone feels appreciated and motivated to do their best.

Trust Over Micromanagement

Now, let's talk about trust.

Remember when someone gave you an important responsibility and said, "I trust you"?

That feeling? It's powerful. It makes you feel like you can move mountains.

Trust over micromanagement is about stepping back and giving your team the space to make decisions.

Micromanaging might produce short-term results, but suffocates creativity and builds resentment over time.

Leaders with high RQ understand that trust is a two-way street: when you trust your team, they thrive.

As leadership expert Jon Gordon (2007) emphasizes, the best teams are fueled by trust, positivity, and empowerment, not fear or control.

Trust creates momentum. Positivity sustains it. Empowerment multiplies it.

Think about a time when you felt trusted. How did it change the way you performed?

You gave it your all, didn't you? Because you felt valued.

The secret sauce of exceptional leadership isn't micromanagement — it's trust.

When you believe in your team and give them space to shine, they will often exceed your highest expectations.

> Trust creates momentum.
> Positivity sustains it.
> Empowerment multiplies it.

Communication That Inspires

Finally, let's talk about communication. Have you ever talked with a leader who felt more like a distant authority figure than a real person? And then, there's the leader who made you feel like your voice mattered—like they genuinely listened.

Communication That Inspires is about creating a dialogue, not just a monologue. It's about asking questions, showing care, listening to the answers, and creating a space where ideas flow freely.

Think about a conversation with a leader who genuinely listened to you. It felt good, didn't it? Trust deepens when communication is open and meaningful, and the team becomes more cohesive. The best leaders don't just talk—they listen and invite collaboration.

By embracing these pillars, leaders create an environment where trust, connection, and open communication are at the forefront, empowering their teams to reach their full potential.

What is Relational Intelligence?

Relationships aren't just a part of leadership—they are the foundation. Whether you're leading a team, guiding students, or fostering a community, everything hinges on how well you connect with the people around you. That's the power of Relational Intelligence: it shifts the focus from tasks and outcomes to the people who will make those outcomes happen.

So what does it look like to lead with RQ? Let's break it down.

The Traits of a Relationally Intelligent Leader

- **Communicating to Connect**: Leaders with high RQ know that effective communication is more than just giving instructions or delivering information. It's about connecting with the people you're talking to. It means listening actively, responding thoughtfully, and being intentional about communicating. You speak with empathy and don't just talk—you listen. You know that authentic leadership begins when communication is a two-way street.

- **Being Other-Focused**: Relationally intelligent leaders focus on others, not themselves. They understand their role is to lift those around them, inspire, and empower. Instead of leading from a place of ego, they lead from a place of service. They focus on the needs, strengths, and growth of others. They're always asking, How can I help you? What can I do to make this better for you? This mindset builds trust and fosters a sense of belonging.

- **Empathy and Emotional Awareness**: At the heart of RQ is empathy—the ability to recognize and understand the feelings of others. Relationally intelligent leaders don't just hear what people say; they know how they feel. They tune into the emotional undercurrents in a room and use that awareness to guide their decisions and actions. This emotional awareness is crucial for creating a supportive and resilient environment where people feel safe to be themselves.

- **Adaptability and Flexibility**: Much like a chef adapts to the ingredients and situation at hand, a leader with strong Relational Intelligence adapts to the needs of their team. They read the room and make adjustments on the fly. They're flexible in their approach, understanding that every situation is unique and requires a thoughtful, tailored response. This ability to pivot and be responsive turns a good leader into a great one.

- **Building Trust and Respect**: Trust is the bedrock of any meaningful relationship, and it's no different in leadership. Relational intelligence involves consistently demonstrating integrity, transparency, and reliability. Leaders with Relational Intelligence know that trust isn't something you demand—you earn it, day in and day out. They are reliable, keep their promises, and act authentically.

How to Build RQ: Actionable Steps for Everyday Leadership

Building Relational Intelligence is a journey—a process, like perfecting that secret sauce. Every step is an ingredient that adds richness to your leadership style. Ready to roll up your sleeves and dive in? Here are five actionable steps to boost your RQ every day:

1. **Practice Active Listening**
   - Focus Fully: Put down your phone, make eye contact, be present, and hear what's being said.
   - Engage Deeply: Ask questions like, "Tell me more about that!" to show interest.
   - Confirm Understanding: Repeat what you've heard to ensure you're on the same page.

2. **Show Appreciation Regularly**
   - Recognize Effort: Celebrate the work behind every accomplishment, not just the outcome.
   - Personalize Praise: Instead of saying, "Good job," say, "I loved how you handled that challenge."
   - Mix It Up: Make appreciation part of your routine in a meeting or a one-on-one.

3. **Be Transparent and Honest**
   - Own Your Mistakes: No one's perfect. When you mess up, own it and turn it into a learning moment. Show your vulnerability. It encourages others to do the same.
   - Share the Big Picture: Let your team in on the big decisions and challenges. The more they know, the more they can contribute.
   - Invite Feedback: Create a space where honest feedback is welcomed and appreciated. Act on the feedback you receive to show your commitment.

4. **Invest in Relationships Daily**
   - One-on-Ones Matter: Make time for regular check-ins that go beyond just work.
   - Foster Informal Connections: Don't wait for meetings. Grab a coffee or chat informally to build rapport.
   - Be Approachable: Make sure your team knows they can come to you anytime.

5. **Model the Behavior You Want to See**
   - Lead by Example: Demonstrate the creativity, respect, and empathy you want to see in your team.

- Show Empathy: Approach challenges with understanding and calm.
- Stay Consistent: Your consistency builds trust over time. Your team will mirror your behaviors.

Why RQ Matters More Than Ever

We live in a time of constant change—teachers are burned out, turnover is high, and pressure is at an all-time peak. But the truth remains: people leave bad leadership, not bad jobs.

Morale plummets when your team feels like just another brick in the wall. But when they feel heard, respected, and trusted? That's when the magic happens.

> We live in a time of constant change... but the truth remains: people leave bad leadership, not bad jobs.

Relational Intelligence isn't just a "nice-to-have"—it's a "must-have." It's the difference between a culture where people show up just to clock in and a place where everyone is excited to contribute and grow.

A Story of Transformation: From Athlete to School Leader

I realize how much my experiences as a student-athlete shaped my understanding and practice of Relational Intelligence. The time I spent on the track with teammates working toward a common goal taught me invaluable lessons about human connections and the importance of navigating interpersonal dynamics.

When I first joined the track team in high school, I focused on the 100-meter hurdles. It was tough, and I fell a lot. One day, after tripping over hurdle after hurdle and landing flat on my face, I could hear my teammates gasping. But my coach's voice rose above it all: "Get back up!" I did. I dusted myself off and tried again. That moment taught me resilience and the importance of adapting quickly to setbacks, essential parts of relational intelligence.

By the time I was competing at Division I, the stakes were higher. But instead of focusing only on my performance, I made it a point to support my teammates. One race, I joked with a teammate about loosening up before the race, saying, "If I hit a hurdle, let's pretend it's part of my strategy to distract the competition." That humor lightened the mood and reminded me that success isn't only about individual achievement—it's about building an environment of trust and camaraderie.

Fast forward to my role as a school leader, and those lessons continue to influence how I lead. Many teachers were overwhelmed when we rolled out a new district-wide reading initiative. One veteran teacher, in particular, voiced her skepticism. Instead of dismissing her concerns, I used my relational intelligence to support her. "I know this is a big shift," I said, "but I also know how much your students respect you. What if we tried just one small step?" The teacher was willing to try one part of the program, trusting that support would be offered every step of the way. What followed turned into a success, and it reminded me how important it is to meet people where they are, recognize their strengths, and foster a supportive environment for growth.

Bringing It All Together: Your Journey to RQ Excellence

Leadership is about creating a space where everyone feels motivated to bring their best selves. Relationship Intelligence, connection, trust, and inspiring communication are at the heart of that transformation.

Your Invitation

This book isn't a one-size-fits-all formula. It's about finding your unique leadership style, trying new things, and building connections that matter. Whether you're a seasoned pro or just getting started, the tools in this book will help you grow into the leader you're meant to be.

So, are you ready to stop being a cook and start being a chef who creates magic? Let's infuse your leadership with authenticity, empathy, and creativity. Together, we'll create something truly special.

CHAPTER TWO
Leading with Authenticity: Being Real

We've all seen it—the leader who checks all the boxes and performs excellently but never truly connects. It may look impressive, but it feels empty. The truth is, **authenticity** transforms leadership from a role to a relationship.

Authenticity is the foundation of trust, and trust is the foundation of loyalty. But here's the real challenge: How do we lead authentically in a world that often demands perfection? The answer lies in vulnerability—showing up as our authentic selves, flaws and all, and letting our team see that we're human too.

I had the privilege of mentoring a superintendent who learned this lesson hard. We met at a local coffee shop on a crisp autumn morning. As we sat, he shared with me his challenges as a leader. He was brilliant, driven, and had grand ideas for improving his district. Yet, despite his best efforts, he struggled to connect with his staff.

He had tried showing appreciation for his teachers, staff, and administrators. On the surface, his efforts seemed thoughtful, but they lacked warmth and sincerity. It was as if he was trying to ride a bike for the first time—he had the right intentions, but the execution wasn't quite there. He wanted his staff to feel valued, but something was missing. There was a disconnect.

Sitting across from him, I could feel his frustration. He genuinely cared for his staff and wanted them to feel appreciated. He asked for advice, and I could tell he was ready for change.

I told him what I believed was the missing piece to his leadership puzzle.

"Educators—whether they're teachers, administrators, or support staff—want a leader who is real with them. They don't expect you to be perfect but want you to be authentic. They need to see that you're human, that you're vulnerable, and that you're actively working on being the best leader you can be. Authenticity builds trust, and trust builds loyalty."

I encouraged him to be open about his struggles. At the next district meeting, I suggested he stand before his team and say something like this: "I know I'm not always the best at showing appreciation in the little ways. I sometimes struggle with it; if you've noticed, I'm not offended by it. But I want you to know I'm working on it. I'm committed to getting better at recognizing all the great things you do."

He hesitated. "But won't that make me look weak? Shouldn't I be showing more confidence as a leader?"

I smiled. "Showing vulnerability doesn't make you weak—it makes you relatable. It shows your team that you're not trying to be perfect but genuinely invested in improving and connecting. They'll appreciate your honesty and respect you more for it."

A few weeks later, he called me with an update. At the district meeting, he took a deep breath and shared the message we had discussed. He admitted to his challenges in showing appreciation and promised his team he was committed to improving. The response was overwhelmingly positive. His staff appreciated his honesty, and many thanked him for being open and vulnerable.

> When we show up as our true selves—imperfections and all—we invite our teams to do the same.

That moment marked a turning point in his leadership. From then on, he became more intentional about showing appreciation authentically through small gestures, thoughtful notes, and moments of genuine connection. The trust and loyalty in his district grew stronger, and he continued to develop more meaningful relationships with his team.

This story is a testament to the power of authentic leadership. When we show up as our true selves—imperfections and all—we invite our teams to do the same. Through these genuine connections, we can build a foundation of trust that will carry our leadership through any challenge.

Authentic vs. Performative Leadership

The difference between authentic and performative leadership is striking, yet often subtle. Authentic leaders are grounded in their values, and their actions align with who they are. They build relationships based on trust, empathy, and mutual respect. They don't shy away from showing vulnerability, admitting mistakes, or seeking feedback to grow. In doing so, they create a culture of openness where their team feels valued and heard.

Performative leadership, in contrast, is driven by the need to project a particular image or meet external expectations. These leaders often prioritize what looks good on the surface over what is genuinely needed. They may wear the mask of confidence, perfection, or strength, but beneath that façade, there is often a disconnect. Their actions may be calculated and designed more to impress or gain approval than to build genuine relationships.

Adults can sense when someone is being authentic versus when they are performing. It's something that's not always easy to define, but it's noticeable. This is why authentic leadership needs to be worked on and continually improved. If we're not mindful of our actions and intentions, we can slip into performative habits without realizing it. The danger of performative leadership is that it may temporarily garner respect or admiration, but doesn't create lasting trust. When leaders only show what they think others want to see—an image of perfection, confidence, or infallibility—it becomes difficult for their teams to connect with them genuinely. People can sense the difference, and that disconnect can lead to disengagement, lack of loyalty, and even turnover over time.

Authentic leadership, on the other hand, thrives on honesty and transparency. It isn't about being perfect; it's about being real. When leaders embrace their humanity and show they have challenges to overcome, they allow their teams to see their growth and journey. This openness fosters a culture of trust, where everyone feels safe to express their ideas, concerns, and mistakes.

A key component of authenticity is vulnerability. It's about letting go of the need to always appear in control or "on top." Instead, authentic leaders acknowledge their imperfections and use those moments as opportunities to connect with their teams. This doesn't mean sharing every personal struggle, but being open enough to show you are human and on a continuous growth journey.

Ultimately, authenticity in leadership is about leading from the heart, not the image. When leaders choose to be themselves—flaws, strengths, and all—they create an environment where others feel safe to do the same. This fosters trust, loyalty, and a deeper connection, leading to more meaningful results.

Tip: When preparing for a meeting or an interaction, take a moment to reflect on your true feelings and thoughts about the topic. Ask yourself: "What do I believe about this?" and "How can I naturally communicate that?"

The Core of Authentic Leadership

To lead with authenticity, you need to build your leadership on four key things: self-awareness, integrity, vulnerability, and transparency. Let's break these down.

Self-Awareness

Self-awareness is the foundation of authentic leadership. It means knowing your strengths, weaknesses, values, and emotions—and understanding how these impact your interactions with others. Self-aware leaders are not afraid to reflect on their actions, accept feedback, and adjust. They are constantly in tune with their inner selves and their external impact.

Strategies to Enhance Self-Awareness:

- **Journaling**: Dedicate a few minutes at the end of each day to reflect on what went well and what didn't. Write down your emotions, reactions, and thoughts. Over time, this practice helps you see patterns and areas for growth.
- **360-Degree Feedback**: 360-Degree Feedback involves gathering input from a variety of sources—colleagues, staff, supervisors, and even students—to provide a well-rounded view of a leader's performance. This method offers valuable insights into how others perceive a leader's strengths and areas for growth, fostering greater self-awareness. When used regularly, 360-degree feedback can help leaders identify blind spots and improve their effectiveness. Research by Smither, London, and Reilly (2005) shows that 360-degree feedback is most effective when part of an ongoing development process, helping leaders align self-perception with others' views.
- **Mindfulness Practices**: Techniques such as meditation or deep breathing exercises can help you center yourself and increase awareness of your reactions and feelings.

Integrity

Integrity means doing the right thing, even when no one is watching. It's about aligning your actions with your values and consistently making decisions. For leaders, integrity is not just a personal virtue—it's a critical component of trust-building. When your staff sees that you stand by your principles, they are more likely to follow suit.

Strategies to Cultivate Integrity:

- **Define Your Values**: Clearly articulate the values that guide you as a leader. Write them down and share them with your team. This can serve as your moral compass in challenging situations.
- **Consistency is Key**: Make sure your actions reflect your words. When staff see consistency in your values and actions, they will know exactly what to expect.
- **Admit Mistakes**: Nobody's perfect. When you make a mistake, acknowledge it openly and share what you've learned from it. This demonstrates that integrity includes accountability.

Vulnerability

Vulnerability is often seen as a weakness, but it is one of the greatest strengths in leadership. Showing vulnerability means being open about your challenges, uncertainties, and failures. It creates a safe space for others to do the same. When you reveal your human side, you invite your team to share their stories, fostering a deeper connection and mutual support.

Strategies to Embrace Vulnerability:
- **Share Personal Stories**: Don't be afraid to talk about moments when you struggled or learned something valuable from a setback. These stories can be powerful lessons for your team.
- **Encourage Open Dialogue**: Create opportunities for your staff to share their challenges without fear of judgment. This can be through informal check-ins, team meetings, or anonymous feedback sessions.
- **Model Risk-Taking**: Let your team see you taking calculated risks and stepping outside your comfort zone. When they see you embracing vulnerability, they'll be more inclined to do the same.

Transparency

Transparency is about openness and honesty in communication. It means sharing your team's successes and challenges. When you are transparent, you create an environment of trust where everyone feels informed and included in the decision-making process.

Strategies to Enhance Transparency:
- **Regular Updates**: Keep your team informed about the big picture and the small details affecting their work. Consistency is key, whether it's a quarterly newsletter or an informal chat.
- **Open Meetings**: Encourage open forums where staff can ask questions and express concerns. This not only builds trust but also ensures that everyone is on the same page.
- **Clear Communication**: Be clear about your expectations, decisions, and rationale. When people understand why decisions are made, they're more likely to support them.

Authenticity is a Journey, Not a Destination

You've probably heard the phrase, "Be yourself." While that's sound advice, authentic leadership demands a bit more. Simply "being yourself" isn't enough if it doesn't involve striving to be your best self. Authenticity in leadership means leveraging your unique talents and continuously growing to bring the highest version of yourself to the table.

Key Concept: Be your authentic self and bring your best talents.

Many leaders settle into a comfort zone by simply being who they are, without pushing for excellence or growth. However, authenticity isn't a static state; it's a dynamic process. It means recognizing that while your true self is valuable, there is always room to grow, develop, and fine-tune your innate talents. When you combine self-acceptance with a commitment to personal and professional growth, you create a leadership style that is both genuine and exceptional.

> Authenticity isn't a static state; it's a dynamic process.

One of the best ways to lead authentically is to seek feedback from our staff, students, and community members. On the surface, it may sound strange to suggest that a leader ask for input from those not in a higher level of authority, but this simple act separates good leaders from great leaders. When was the last time you, as a leader, encouraged your staff to give you genuine and honest feedback on your performance at work?

As a new principal, only a few months into my first year in this role, I wanted to do things right. I had spent years in the classroom and knew how much teachers and staff appreciated feeling heard. So, I invited my entire staff—including teachers, paraprofessionals, custodians, and support personnel—to give me honest, anonymous feedback.

The survey was simple, just three open-ended questions:

- What is going well?
- What are my areas for improvement?
- Is there anything else you want to tell me?

I took a deep breath and clicked "send." The survey was now live for all 130 staff members. That night, I barely slept. Would anyone even respond? Would the comments be constructive or just a laundry list of complaints? The following day, responses started trickling in. Then, they picked up speed. Each time I checked, more feedback had been submitted. It was exhilarating—and terrifying. I waited until the end of the week to read through them. Sitting at my desk, I opened the responses, preparing myself for the worst.

The Feedback

To my relief, the first few responses were overwhelmingly positive. Teachers appreciated my visibility in the hallways and classrooms. Support staff noted that I had taken time to learn their names and listen to their concerns. The custodial team mentioned how they felt valued when I acknowledged their hard work. Then came the constructive feedback. Some teachers wished for more straightforward communication on expectations. A few staff members suggested I delegate more, noting that I was taking on too much myself. Others encouraged me to be more decisive in handling conflicts. None of it was cruel or mean-spirited—just honest reflections from people who wanted our school to be the best it could be.

One response stood out to me: "Thank you for asking us. No principal has ever done this before." That was all it said. Short, simple, and powerful.

The Ripple Effect

The following week, I addressed the feedback in our staff meeting. I shared the major takeaways—what we were doing well and where I could improve. I clarified that I was listening, and their words weren't going into a void. I even asked for volunteers to help brainstorm solutions for some of the concerns they raised.

The response was incredible. Staff members stopped me in the hallways to say they appreciated the transparency. A veteran teacher said she wished her previous principals had done something similar. A paraprofessional admitted she had hesitated to submit feedback but was glad she did after hearing how I took it seriously.

Over time, something unexpected happened. Because I had modeled openness to feedback, my staff started embracing it, too. Teachers began asking their students for input on lessons. Department leads initiated peer observations to exchange constructive suggestions. The school culture started shifting from one of quiet frustrations to one of open dialogue and continuous improvement.

Looking back, sending that survey was one of the most vulnerable things I had ever done as a leader. But it was also one of the most rewarding. So, to those new to the role, those who have been in leadership for years, and those who aspire to one day lead—I encourage you to try this. Create your own 100-Day Administrator Feedback Survey. Ask your staff what's working, where you can improve, and what else they want you to know. Then, listen. Not just to praise, but to the areas of growth. Take action where you can.

When leaders are willing to learn and grow, it creates a ripple effect. Teachers, staff, and students begin to mirror that same mindset. Ultimately, that's how schools improve—not through top-down mandates, but through a culture of trust, collaboration, and continuous learning.

Deepening the Connection Between Authenticity and Organizational Impact

Authentic leadership benefits the individual leader and has a profound, positive impact on the entire organization. When leaders exhibit authenticity, they foster an environment that thrives on trust, engagement, and growth. Research has shown that authentic leadership improves retention rates, morale, and overall school performance.

According to a 2022 leadership study, 80% of employees reported feeling more engaged when their leaders exhibited authentic qualities (Leadership Circle, as cited in Vorecol). Additionally, authentic leaders inspire and motivate subordinates to achieve goals through authenticity and positive moral views, aided by enhanced awareness and effective communication (Crawford et al., 2019).

This research highlights that authentic leadership is crucial in shaping personal leadership growth and cultivating success across the school community.

Actionable Steps:

- **Self-Reflection**: Regularly assess who you are and who you aspire to be. Identify your core talents and consider how you can further develop them.
- **Professional Development**: Invest in courses, workshops, or coaching that can help you hone your skills. Whether it's public speaking, strategic thinking, or creative problem-solving, continuously improving your talents elevates your authenticity.
- **Goal Setting**: Set personal and professional goals that challenge you to grow. Align these goals with your values so that your journey toward excellence remains true to who you are.
- **Feedback Loop**: Create a culture of feedback, both giving and receiving. Understanding how others perceive your strengths can help you further develop them.

Remember, being authentic isn't just about being comfortable in your skin—it's about actively cultivating and showcasing the best parts of yourself so that you can inspire and lead others more effectively.

Tips and Strategies for Exceptional Authentic Leadership

As you work on developing your authentic leadership style, keep these additional tips and strategies in mind:

- **Practice Active Listening**: Make it a habit to listen more than speak. Ask open-ended questions and show genuine curiosity about your team's perspectives.
- **Lead by Example**: Your behavior sets the standard. Demonstrate vulnerability, integrity, and a commitment to continual improvement, and your team will follow suit.
- **Celebrate Successes and Failures**: Recognize that every outcome is an opportunity to learn—frame mistakes as valuable lessons rather than failures.
- **Maintain Balance**: Authenticity doesn't mean oversharing. Find a balance between being open and maintaining professional boundaries.
- **Stay Curious and Invest in Yourself**: Continuously seek new knowledge and perspectives. Attend workshops, read widely, and engage in conversations that challenge your thinking.
- **Foster a Culture of Feedback**: Encourage your team to share their thoughts about your leadership. This will help you grow and reinforce a culture of mutual respect and continuous improvement.

Conclusion: Embracing Your Authentic Leadership Journey

Leading with authenticity isn't a destination—it's a lifelong journey. As you embrace the unique strengths, vulnerabilities, and talents that make you exceptional, you'll find that authentic leadership naturally fosters trust, collaboration, and innovation within your school community. Remember, being genuine is not simply about "being yourself" but striving to be your best self by developing and sharing your unique talents.

By distinguishing yourself from performative leadership and building your style on the pillars of self-awareness, integrity, vulnerability, and transparency while committing to continuous growth, you set the stage for a dynamic, supportive, and engaged school culture. As you develop your personal leadership manifesto, you create a clear, actionable guide that reminds you of who you are and aspire to be, even during challenging times.

I invite you to take these ideas, experiment with them in your day-to-day leadership, and share your experiences with your team. Authentic leadership is contagious. When you show up as your true, ever-improving self, you inspire others to do the same, creating a ripple effect that transforms your entire educational community.

Embrace your authenticity, lead confidently, and remember: your genuine commitment to being your best authentic self sets you apart as an exceptional leader.

Leadership in Action: Developing Your Personal Leadership Manifesto

Creating a personal leadership manifesto helps you lead authentically by defining your values, goals, and principles. It serves as a guide for your actions and sets clear expectations for your staff. Here's how to develop one:

Step 1: Reflect on Your Values and Experiences

Reflect on the values guiding your decisions and the key moments shaping your leadership. Journal your thoughts or discuss them with a colleague for clarity.

Step 2: Identify the Pillars of Your Authentic Leadership

Identify core pillars like self-awareness, integrity, vulnerability, and transparency, which will form the foundation of your manifesto.

Step 3: Articulate Your Vision and Goals

Outline your leadership vision, focusing on the culture, relationships, and outcomes you want to create. Use vivid language to describe what you aspire to achieve.

Step 4: Write Your Manifesto

Combine your values, pillars, and vision into a compelling draft. This manifesto is your commitment to leading with authenticity and empowerment.

Step 5: Share and Refine

Seek feedback from a mentor or colleague to refine your manifesto. Once satisfied, consider sharing it with your team to set the tone for transparent leadership.

Step 6: Define Your Non-Negotiables and Commit to Supporting Your Staff

Identify principles you'll never compromise on, such as support, honesty, accountability, and excellence. Include these in your manifesto to show your commitment to leadership and staff well-being.

Step 7: Revisit and Revise Regularly

Your manifesto should evolve. Regularly revisit and revise it to stay aligned with your values and adapt to new challenges, ensuring it remains an effective tool for your leadership journey.

Remember: Incorporating a personal leadership manifesto into your practice empowers you to lead with purpose and integrity. By reflecting on your values, defining the pillars of your leadership, and committing to continuous growth, you create a clear roadmap for yourself and your team. This manifesto serves as a guiding document for your leadership journey and sets the tone for a supportive, transparent, and empowering environment for your staff. Revisit and refine it regularly to ensure your leadership evolves alongside your challenges and successes. Ready to lead authentically and impactfully? Start crafting your manifesto today and inspire those around you to do the same!

CHAPTER THREE
Trust Capital: The Currency of Leadership

Imagine you walk into a staff meeting, and something feels off. The energy is low. Teachers nod politely, but their engagement is surface-level. Decisions take longer, collaboration feels forced, and there's hesitation. What's missing? Trust.

Without trust, leadership flounders. It's like trying to lead a team without a shared language—nothing works smoothly. According to Stephen M.R. Covey (2006), author of *The Speed of Trust*, trust is the "single most overlooked and underutilized asset in business and leadership." When trust is present, everything flows—decisions are made faster, communication is more effective, and teams work better together. Without it, the opposite happens.

> Trust doesn't happen by accident. You have to build, nurture, and sustain it, or it can be depleted like money in the bank.

Trust is the foundation of all successful leadership. The invisible force keeps everything together, motivating your team and creating an environment where everyone can thrive. But here's the thing—trust doesn't happen by accident. You have to build, nurture, and sustain it, or it can be depleted like money in the bank.

Trust, like currency, can be drained if you're not careful. Many leaders find themselves in a position where their trust bank is empty—or worse, in the red—and they don't even realize it. According to Brene Brown (2018), in her book *Dare to Lead*, trust is not just a "nice-to-have" but a "must-have" to create a culture where people feel safe, seen, and supported.

What is Trust Capital?

Trust Capital is the currency of leadership. Think of it like a bank account. You make deposits every time you follow through on your promises, show up for your team, or make thoughtful, transparent decisions. But if you miss meetings, fail to follow through on commitments, or make decisions without transparency, you're making withdrawals.

And here's the thing: you're in trouble if you withdraw too much without making regular deposits. A leader in the red with trust might not notice it immediately. They might think everything is fine, but people stop following their lead over time. They disengage from their work or even start to distrust their decisions. Suddenly, there's a shift in the culture, and things begin to feel off.

Signs Your Trust Bank is in the Red:

- You make decisions without input and expect compliance.
- You are visible only during crises, not during day-to-day operations.
- You announce significant changes without explaining why or consulting those affected.
- Your team hesitates to speak up in meetings.

Some leaders don't realize they've drained their trust balance. They may be managing from behind their desks, only showing up when things are going well, or making promises but never following through. Gradually, their trust account is depleted, and they remain unaware of the damage being done.

Eventually, the effects catch up. Staff stop speaking up, engagement decreases, and the culture becomes tense. People are no longer motivated to go the extra mile. They begin to disengage.

Think about a leader you've encountered who was "in the red" with trust. What did their actions look like? Did they lack follow-through? Were they unavailable or disengaged? Over time, that lack of trust erodes morale and success.

Here's the challenge: If you keep withdrawing from your trust bank without making regular deposits, you'll become isolated and disconnected from your team. You must monitor your trust balance and ask yourself: *How much trust do I have in the bank right now? Am I spending more than I'm investing?*

Small Talk, Big Impact: The Key to Building Trust

Building your trust bank doesn't require grand gestures—it's about small, intentional actions that show your team you care about them as people, not just employees.

When discussing trust capital, getting caught up in significant organizational changes is easy. But often, the most effective trust-building actions are the little things. Small talk, showing genuine interest, and taking the time to learn about your staff's lives go a long way toward creating a culture of trust.

Start with the Person, Not the Task

One of the most potent ways to build trust is by showing interest in your staff as people, not just employees. Ask about their families, their interests, and their passions. Show up to events where they'll be and chat with them about more than just work.

By making these small deposits into your trust bank, you're letting your staff know you see them as whole people. You value them for more than their professional contributions, and that alone can go a long way in building trust.

Be Consistent with Your Actions

Consistency is key to trust. Imagine being a warm and friendly leader one day but distant the next. Your team will wonder which version of you they will get. This unpredictability can erode trust over time.

Instead, focus on being consistently present. Show up to meetings prepared, follow through on your commitments, and ensure that your support isn't just a one-time thing but a regular part of your leadership style. Trust grows over time, but only when you're consistent with your actions.

Try This: Pick one leadership habit to refine and stick with it. Maybe it's always greeting your staff in the morning or checking in with each team member weekly. These small, consistent actions will help you build a foundation of trust that you can continue to build on.

Listen Like You Mean It

Listening is one of the most powerful tools for building trust. But too often, leaders listen to fix things or, worse, just to respond. Real listening is about hearing people and understanding their perspective before jumping to conclusions.

When a staff member comes to you with concerns or ideas, give them your full attention. Ask questions to understand their point of view and offer feedback that shows you've heard them.

Try This: When a staff member expresses concern, resist the urge to jump in with solutions immediately. Instead, ask them, "What would help you feel better about this situation?" or "What can I do to support you?"

You build trust and rapport by showing genuine interest in their thoughts and feelings. Over time, that will make a massive difference in how your team perceives you and how willing they are to be open with you in the future.

Replenishing the Trust Bank: Recognizing When You're in the Red

Mistakes, missed deadlines, and tough decisions will happen. What matters is how you repair trust when it's broken. Recognizing when your trust bank is red is essential to maintaining a high-performing team. Proactively repairing trust when withdrawals occur can prevent lasting damage to relationships.

If you've made a mistake, own it. If you've let someone down, acknowledge it and take steps to make it right. Leaders who take responsibility for their actions and work to restore trust foster an environment of honesty and humility, strengthening their teams. Rebuilding trust is about resolving the issue at hand and reaffirming your commitment to the relationship.

Try This: Reflect on your recent leadership actions. Are there any areas where you've made withdrawals without replenishing? Whether offering a heartfelt apology, publicly acknowledging your mistake, or simply showing up more consistently, there are always ways to rebuild trust.

The Ripple Effect of Trust

Building trust isn't just about improving your team or school; it has a ripple effect that extends far beyond your immediate circle. When your staff trusts you, they are more likely to trust each other. This fosters collaboration, sparks creativity, and promotes innovation. When students feel trust among their teachers, they feel safer, more engaged, and ready to take risks in their learning.

The best part? Trust is contagious. It spreads from person to person, creating a culture of respect, collaboration, and mutual support.

As a new leader at my school, I quickly noticed that our leadership team had all the right pieces—a talented assistant principal and dedicated department chairs—but something was missing. The conversations were productive, yet they lacked a personal connection. I realized we couldn't unlock our full potential as a team without trust.

To address this, I focused on team-building efforts—no icebreakers or trust falls, but authentic opportunities for us to connect personally. Our first attempt was a structured book study on group dynamics, followed by personality assessments and communication strategies. While valuable, the real breakthrough happened unexpectedly.

One afternoon, after a draining meeting about school improvement goals, I casually said, "I could go for some chocolate right now."

Without missing a beat, our math instructional coach responded, "Oh! You HAVE to try my homemade chocolate brownies. They'll change your life!"

That one offhand comment sparked a lively, 20-minute discussion about brownies—fudgy versus cakey, corner versus center, walnuts or no walnuts (for me, no nuts), and even frosting vs. plain. The conversation quickly evolved into a debate about the best desserts in general. We learned about our assistant principal's obsession with frozen peanut butter cups and our instructional team leader's claims of making the best cheesecake in town.

Our math coach brought in a tray of her famous brownies the following week, and "Dessert Fridays" were born. Each Friday, a different team member brought in a favorite dessert to share. It became a lighthearted ritual that everyone looked forward to, offering a break from the stresses of school leadership.

What began as casual conversations about sweets led to genuine personal connections. We talked about our families, weekend plans, and funny teaching moments. And that trust began to flow into our professional work. By the time the school year was in full swing, the team felt completely different. Meetings were easier, and collaboration came naturally—people who had hesitated to ask for help now reached out without hesitation. The sense of trust transformed how we worked together.

This experience mirrors the findings of Gallup's research on trust in the workplace, which reveals that trust has a significant impact on team engagement, retention, and productivity. When trust is high, teams are more likely to collaborate, be productive, and remain engaged with their work (Gallup, 2020). Trust isn't just a feel-good factor; it's the backbone of high-performing teams.

Fostering trust can create a positive cycle that fuels innovation, enhances team morale, and ultimately drives success. Trust isn't just a foundational value; it's an operational necessity.

Implementing Aspirational Conversations (With Reflective Questions)

One of the most powerful tools I used as an administrator was something I called aspirational conversations. One of the best ways to build a culture of trust and empowerment is by asking the right questions that encourage reflection, open dialogue, and mutual growth. I introduced these conversations into regular check-ins and ensured they were integrated into our evaluation process. This allowed the conversation to be a two-way dialogue rather than a one-way evaluation. Including reflective questions during evaluations helped my staff engage in their development by reflecting on their needs and aspirations, which deepened our connection and strengthened our culture of trust.

Create Regular Check-ins:

Schedule consistent one-on-one or small group meetings focusing on long-term professional goals and aspirations. This should be more than just a catch-up on tasks—it's a chance for reflection. To kickstart these conversations, try these open-ended questions:

- "What do we do well as a school/district/team?"
- "What areas do you think we can improve on?"
- "How can we improve the work environment for you and your colleagues?"
- "What can I do as your leader to support your goals?"

By including these questions in evaluations, the process became an opportunity for staff to express their individual needs and contributions. When staff are invited to reflect on these questions and their professional growth, it's no longer just a performance review but a meaningful dialogue. Taking this input and actively working to meet their needs is a powerful way to build trust and foster a positive culture within the team. Their insights are valued, and the feedback they provide directly influences change.

Ask About Growth and Aspirations:

When you ask staff about their future and growth, you see them as professionals with dreams, not just employees completing tasks.

While focusing on day-to-day operations is essential, you also want to create space for teachers to think big and share their long-term career goals. Here are questions to guide these conversations:

- "Where do you see yourself in the next few years? What's one area you'd like to grow in?"
- "What professional development opportunities would help you achieve your career goals?"
- "Is there a role or responsibility that excites you? How can we help you move toward that?"

Including these questions in evaluations allowed for discussions about personal and professional aspirations. When you ask staff about their future and growth, you see them as professionals with dreams, not just employees completing tasks. Their answers provided invaluable insights into how I, as a leader, could align their development with both their aspirations and the school's evolving needs. This allowed me to better support them in meeting their goals, creating a stronger, more motivated team.

Ask About Organizational Improvement:

Teachers must know that their feedback leads to positive change to make these conversations meaningful. You open up a two-way dialogue that encourages trust-building by asking them what the organization does well and what can be improved. Try asking:

- "What do you think we do well as a team? What sets us apart?"
- "What do you think we could improve on as an organization? What changes would make the biggest difference?"
- "How do you think we can work together to strengthen the culture of trust here?"

Including questions about organizational improvement within the evaluation dialogue fosters ownership and investment in the team's success. When teachers know their feedback is taken seriously and leads to change, it helps build an environment of trust and collective growth. It's not about a top-down directive but about coming together to strengthen the entire team's culture.

Addressing Concerns with Positivity:

Fostering an optimistic mindset in these conversations is essential even when staff members express challenges or concerns. You can use reflective questioning to reframe problems into opportunities for growth. For example:

- "I understand there are challenges around [issue], but I'm curious—how do you think we could approach this differently?"
- "What solutions do you think might work, and how can I support you in implementing them?"

By incorporating these questions into evaluations, I ensured the focus was on solutions rather than just identifying problems. This approach emphasized that the review was about pointing out weaknesses and collaboratively finding ways to overcome challenges. It allowed me to support my staff meaningfully, ensuring they felt heard, valued, and empowered to contribute to solutions, strengthening trust in the leadership and each other.

Creating a Safe Space for Reflection

The goal is to create an environment where reflective conversations feel like an ongoing, safe dialogue. To do this, keep these principles in mind:

- **Be Open and Vulnerable**: Share your reflections as a leader and model the behavior you expect from your team. For example, when you ask, *"What do you think we could do better?"* Be prepared to hear constructive feedback and demonstrate your commitment to improvement by acting on it. This encourages others to be candid in their responses.
- **Follow Up on Feedback**: It's essential to ask these questions and take action on the feedback received. If teachers have suggested an area of improvement, follow up with tangible steps and let them know how their input has shaped decisions. This builds trust and shows that their voices matter.
- **Use the Feedback to Shape Future Conversations**: If recurring themes come up in these conversations, use them as starting points for future discussions. For example, if several teachers need more professional development in a particular area, discuss it in the next conversation and explore solutions together.

Final Thoughts: Bringing Reflective Conversations to Life

Building trust is a journey that requires consistent effort, empathy, and a willingness to engage in open, reflective conversations. By asking questions that encouraging reflection on individual and organizational growth, you can create a culture of transparency, empowerment, and continuous improvement. These conversations provide the foundation for trust because they show that you value your team's input, respect their aspirations, and are committed to supporting their growth.

Remember, the key to these conversations is what you ask and how you listen, act, and follow up. Your goal is to make the process feel authentic and ongoing. When teachers feel heard and supported, they will trust you more and be more motivated to bring their best selves to work daily.

So, start today—ask your staff the questions that matter, listen actively, and turn those insights into action. The results will speak for themselves. You'll see your trust bank balance grow, and more importantly, you'll see a culture where everyone feels valued, empowered, and invested in the school's success.

Transition to Part II
The Communication Pillar

Trust and communication are both pillars of relational intelligence. Now that we've explored the power of trust, we must shift our focus to the second pillar: Communication. These two pillars are inseparable. While trust lays the groundwork for meaningful relationships, communication builds the connections that make those relationships thrive.

As I often say, *"Communication isn't just about being heard—it's about making others feel heard."* This decisive shift in mindset bridges the gap between trust and communication. When we make others feel heard, we validate their experiences and emotions, strengthening trust. Without this emotional connection, trust is fragile at best. But when communication is used to listen and engage genuinely, it becomes the vehicle that drives deeper understanding, collaboration, and respect.

This section will explore how communication goes far beyond simply exchanging words. It's about mastering listening, using non-verbal cues to enhance understanding, and knowing when to set boundaries to maintain healthy relationships. Whether you're speaking with your staff, guiding a student through a difficult moment, or engaging with a concerned parent, your communication must be intentional and empathetic.

> Communication isn't just about being heard—it's about making others feel heard.

Effective communication isn't always easy, especially under pressure. But when done with purpose, it creates a space where people feel safe, understood, and valued. And that's when real change begins.

Building Relationships through Communication

We'll start by identifying the key people in your network: friends, associates, assignments, and advisors. Understanding who you're communicating with and why is the first step toward developing a relationship-building strategy that works for you, your team, and your school. We'll map out these relationships, prioritize where to invest your energy, and focus on the most critical connections.

Next, we'll explore active listening because listening is the true art of communication. It's not just about hearing words; it's about hearing the emotion behind them, the context, and the needs of the person speaking. Mastering this skill creates deeper connections and fosters more authentic conversations.

We'll also explore the power of praise, essential to creating a positive culture. Recognition isn't just nice—it's necessary. People need to feel appreciated, and clear, positive communication helps cultivate a culture where individuals feel valued and motivated.

Finally, we'll discuss the importance of boundaries. Leadership comes with constant demands, but learning to communicate boundaries with yourself and others is key to leading sustainably.

As we move forward, remember: communication isn't just about what you say; it's about how you say it, when you say it, and, most importantly, how you listen. In the upcoming chapters, we'll dive into powerful communication tools that will help you strengthen every relationship in your leadership role.

CHAPTER FOUR
The Power of Relationships

What separates a thriving school culture from one that struggles with disengagement and low morale? It's not policies, programs, or funding—it's relationships. When people feel valued, they give their best. When they don't, they disengage. This isn't just true in education; it's true in every organization, including the military. Take, for example, the USS Benfold...

When Admiral D. Michael Abrashoff took command of the USS Benfold in 1997, he wasn't inheriting just a ship but a broken culture. Sure, the ship was full of cutting-edge technology. But that didn't matter because of the state of the crew. They were disengaged, frustrated, and felt as disconnected as a ship lost at sea. The problem? Leadership. The former captain, although talented, didn't have the relational chops—what we call Relational Intelligence (RQ)—to connect with his people. His leadership style? It was all about rigid commands and cold hierarchies. The result? A crew that felt undervalued and unappreciated led to performance that was just as miserable as morale.

Then, enter Captain Abrashoff. He didn't focus on upgrading tech or restructuring the crew. He focused on something much more powerful: relationships. He famously said, "The best way to lead is to listen to your people, treat them with respect, and empower them to take ownership." This wasn't just about command—it was about connection. He invested in relationships, and the results were mind-blowing. Under his leadership, the Benfold became one of the highest-performing ships in the fleet, not because of fancier gadgets but because of the team's renewed trust and motivation.

And guess what? This lesson isn't just for military leaders. It's a must for educational leaders, too. Whether running a school or a ship, relationships are the foundation of success. The people you lead are what make the systems, programs, and technologies work. When you build trust and foster positive relationships, you create a school that thrives. Just like Captain Abrashoff turned his ship around by prioritizing relationships, school leaders can transform their communities by focusing on four key types of leadership relationships: Personal, Professional, Task-Oriented, and Advisor relationships.

The Four Key Dimensions of Leadership Relationships

Leadership isn't just about keeping things running smoothly; it's about how you connect with the people who make it all happen. As an educational leader, you're constantly navigating relationships with teachers, students, parents, colleagues—you name it. And the truth? It's not just one relationship; it's a whole web of them, each affecting your school's vibe, morale, and performance.

But no need to panic! Instead of juggling a million relationships simultaneously, focus on these four key pillars of leadership relationships: **Friends**, **Associates**, **Assignments**, and **Advisors**. You must nurture these relationships to build trust, boost morale, and create a cohesive school culture. When you focus on these four, you're not just building a school—you're building a community where everyone shows up for each other.

1. Personal Connections: Building Trust Through Humanity

Leadership is about how you make people feel. How do your staff members feel when they walk into your office or down the school hallway? Do they feel seen, heard, and respected? When people know you care about them, not just as employees, but as individuals, they're more likely to go the extra mile for you and the kids they teach.

> When people know you care about them, not just as employees, but as individuals, they're more likely to go the extra mile for you and the kids they teach.

Building these connections doesn't require grand gestures. The little things matter: listening, being present, and showing empathy. When you take the time to connect with your team on a personal level, honestly, they'll know you're in their corner, whether they're battling a complex personal issue or just struggling to keep up with the latest educational trends. And let's be honest: when your staff knows you have their back, they're more likely to stick with you, especially when the going gets tough.

Leadership has always been about people, not just policies, and that belief was tested early in my career as a school leader. One morning, I noticed a typically energetic teacher sitting at his desk, visibly drained. His wife was seriously ill, and he was struggling to balance caregiving, parenting, and the looming report card deadlines. Though he never asked for help, it was clear he needed support.

I extended his deadline and organized a meal train with a colleague's help. The staff's response was overwhelming, and over the next few weeks, his spirit lifted as his wife's health improved. It reminded me that great schools aren't built on policies but on people who show up for each other.

Deadlines were important, but they were not more important than his well-being. He was a dedicated teacher who had always met expectations, and at that moment, he needed grace. The decision to extend his deadline was an easy one. He resisted initially, not wanting special treatment, but he needed to understand that this wasn't about bending rules—it was about support. If any other staff member had been in their shoes, the same would have been done for them.

Even with the extension, it was clear that more needed to be done. He wasn't just behind on work; he was carrying a load that no one should bear alone. A trusted colleague, known for keeping the team connected, immediately recognized how to help. A meal train was the first step—something simple yet meaningful to ease his daily stress. Within hours, she had organized a schedule, and the response from the staff was overwhelming. Teachers, paraprofessionals, and office staff signed up to bring home-cooked meals or provide gift cards to local restaurants.

Over the next few days, the difference was noticeable. As the weeks went by, his wife's condition improved, and so did his spirit. Eventually, he caught up on his work, but more importantly, he knew he wasn't alone. The experience reinforced a truth I've carried with me ever since: great schools aren't built on policies but on people who show up for each other when it matters most.

How to Strengthen Personal Connections:

- **Make Time for Small Talk**: It's not just fluff. Asking someone how their day is going or sharing a funny story builds trust.
- **Practice Active Listening**: Be present. Listen—not just to fix but to understand.
- **Offer Support, Not Just Solutions**: Sometimes, people don't need answers. They just need someone to show they care.

2. Professional Collaborations: Elevating the Collective Through Trust

Personal connections are essential, but collaboration is where the magic happens. Leadership doesn't happen in a vacuum. It thrives on teamwork. As a leader, your job is to create an environment where people feel safe collaborating, sharing ideas, and leaning on each other. But, and here's the catch, trust is key to collaboration. Without it, people will hold back, second-guess themselves, and avoid risk-taking.

Here's a story: I thought I had this whole leadership thing figured out. After years of teaching kindergarten, I felt prepared for anything—until I observed a 5th-grade math lesson. I had no idea what I was looking at. I was totally out of my depth. At that moment, I had to admit, I didn't know what I didn't know.

So, I went to the math coach and asked for help. Instead of pretending to have all the answers, I humbled myself and leaned on her expertise. Together, we collaborated to design professional development that truly met the needs of the 5th-grade team. What happened? Not only did the teachers appreciate that I wasn't trying to be the expert, but they also respected me more. They saw me as one of them, learning alongside them.

The takeaway? Leadership isn't about having all the answers. It's about building trust through humility, fostering collaboration, and creating a culture where everyone feels empowered to learn and grow together. To strengthen professional collaborations, make space for open conversations where everyone can share ideas freely. Celebrate team achievements to reinforce that success is a collective effort. And encourage risk-taking and experimentation—when people feel supported, they're more likely to try new things, even if they don't work out perfectly the first time.

How to Strengthen Professional Collaborations:

- **Facilitate Open Conversations**: Create a space where everyone feels comfortable sharing ideas.
- **Celebrate Team Achievements**: Recognize collaborative successes. It's about celebrating we, not just me.
- **Encourage Risk-Taking and Experimentation**: Don't let fear of failure hold your team back. Support them when they try something new, even if it doesn't happen the first time.

3. Task-Oriented Relationships: Empowering Through Clarity and Autonomy

Relationships are important, but so is making sure everyone knows their role and feels empowered to own it. Clarity and autonomy are key ingredients in this kind of leadership. It's not about micromanaging—it's about setting the stage so your team can step up, take ownership, and shine.

Let me take you back to a story that still cracks me up. Early in my career, we were having a fundraiser at school, and as part of it, we decided to do a "Principal for the Day" raffle. The winner would have a lot of responsibility, needing to decide about the school day and lead the team. This was a task-oriented challenge. I had to ensure the student knew what was expected and then step back and let them make their calls.

When the day finally came, the 5th grader winner was thrilled but also overwhelmed. I gave them the reins, ensured they understood what they were managing, and then stepped back to let them take charge. Guess what happened? They crushed it! They made thoughtful decisions, handled challenges, and even rallied the staff around their initiatives. It wasn't about the power but about clarity, trust, and giving them the autonomy to lead.

That little experience showed me a big lesson: Just like that student, teachers thrive when they have the space to take ownership of their tasks. They rise to the occasion when they understand what's expected of them and trust they can make decisions. Micromanagement erodes trust, but clarity and autonomy empower people to lead at every level. This lesson is as true for adults as it is for students.

How to Strengthen Task-Oriented Relationships:

- **Clarify Expectations**: Be crystal clear about what needs to happen. If your team doesn't know precisely what you want, they'll flounder. So, take the time to be specific and provide the details they need to succeed.
- **Empower Through Autonomy**: Give people the space to take charge. When they feel trusted, they take pride in their work, and their motivation soars.
- **Provide Support, Not Supervision**: Trust your team to do their jobs. Offer guidance when needed, but give them the room to make decisions and learn from their mistakes.

4. Advisor Relationships: Mentorship and Growth

No leader can do it alone. It's crucial to have advisors—people who've been around the block, seen the highs and lows, and can offer some wisdom when needed. These advisor relationships are where the magic happens—they provide perspective, guidance, and emotional support that can make all the difference in a crisis.

I'll never forget when I was thrown into a major leadership challenge. We had a key leadership team member leave unexpectedly, and to make matters worse, it was right before a huge district audit. The pressure was on, and I was unsure how to handle the transition. At that moment, I picked up the phone and called an old mentor of mine—someone who had been a superintendent for years and had seen it all.

I told her, "I don't know how I will get through this." And instead of giving me a laundry list of "do this, do that," she calmly said, "You don't have to have all the answers. What's important is knowing who to turn to for help and being humble enough to ask."

Her advice gave me the clarity I needed. It wasn't about knowing everything—it was about trusting the process, knowing I could rely on others for support, and staying focused on what mattered. With her guidance, I navigated the crisis and led the team through a successful audit. That experience solidified for me just how valuable advisor relationships are for troubleshooting problems and personal and professional growth.

Years later, I found myself in another high-pressure situation, and the memory of my mentor's advice came flooding back. This time, I didn't panic. I remembered that I didn't need all the answers—I needed the right people around me. That mindset shift continued to guide my leadership decisions, reinforcing the importance of humility, collaboration, and trust. My mentor's words became a touchstone in my leadership philosophy, shaping how I approach challenges even today.

How to Strengthen Advisor Relationships:

- **Seek Out Mentors**: Find people who have been through the trenches and can offer solid, experience-based advice. Be proactive about reaching out.
- **Listen and Reflect**: When your mentor talks, listen carefully. It's not just about hearing words—it's about understanding and applying the deeper meaning to your situation.
- **Be Open to Feedback**: We all have room to grow. Don't shy away from honest feedback—it's the only way to improve.

Transforming Leadership Through Relationships

Admiral Abrashoff's success wasn't just about using leadership techniques—it was a shift in mindset. He understood that leadership is about empowering people, not controlling them. This same mindset can transform schools. When leaders prioritize relationships, they create a culture where educators feel valued, students feel supported, and communities feel engaged. These relationships become the cornerstone for school transformation, driving progress and fostering a sense of belonging.

The Ripple Effect of Relational Leadership

When leaders focus on building relationships, the impact reaches far beyond the immediate circle. Strong relationships do more than just improve morale—they create a ripple effect across the entire school community. Teachers who feel respected and supported are more likely to create positive classroom environments, which leads to better student engagement, improved behavior, and academic growth. Similarly, when leaders build trust with parents and the wider community, it creates an environment where the whole school can thrive.

Effective leaders recognize that relational leadership isn't just for immediate results—it builds the foundation for long-term success. When relationships are at the forefront, there's a shared sense of ownership, empowering everyone to give their best.

> Effective leaders recognize that relational leadership isn't just for immediate results—it builds the foundation for long-term success.

Vulnerability in Leadership: The Key to Authenticity

Great leaders embrace vulnerability, not as a weakness but as a path to authenticity. When leaders show vulnerability, they become more human, not just figures of authority. This openness builds trust, and trust strengthens relationships. A trusting team is willing to take risks, share ideas, and support each other through challenges.

As a leader, be authentic. Don't hesitate to admit when you don't have all the answers, and be open to learning from your staff. When your team sees you practicing vulnerability, it creates a safe space for them to do the same. This openness fosters a sense of community, where people feel safe to share their thoughts and challenges without fear of judgment.

The Long-Term Benefits of Relational Leadership

Building relationships takes time, but the payoff is invaluable. Schools led by leaders with relational intelligence tend to see improved teacher retention, better student outcomes, and stronger community involvement. Relationships nurture an environment where innovation flourishes and staff members are deeply committed to the school's mission.

Investing in relationships means investing in growth for both individuals and the school. When leaders nurture relationships at all levels, they open the door to professional development, personal fulfillment, and a shared vision of success. These strong relationships become the driving force for continuous improvement, helping everyone reach their fullest potential.

Final Thought

Educational leaders can transform struggling schools into dynamic, thriving communities. This transformation doesn't come from rigid rules or top-down mandates but through relationships. The best principals, superintendents, and administrators understand that their impact isn't measured by authority, but by the strength of the relationships they build.

By prioritizing personal connections, professional collaborations, task-driven relationships, and mentorship, you'll unlock your team's full potential and create an environment where everyone—teachers, students, and families—feels empowered to succeed.

The key to a successful school is simple: Leadership is Relationships. When relationships are central to leadership, everything else falls into place. People who feel seen, heard, and valued will bring their best selves to work, school, and the community.

So, as you step into your leadership role, remember this: Transform your school by transforming relationships. Build trust, foster collaboration, and empower those around you. The results will be nothing short of remarkable.

Now, ask yourself: How will you strengthen your leadership relationships today?

Best Practices in Action

- **Prioritize Active Listening**: Leaders who truly listen build trust and foster stronger connections. Make it a habit to practice active listening in all your interactions—whether with staff, students, or parents. Show that you're hearing not just the words but also the emotions behind them. Reflect back what you hear and ask follow-up questions to keep the conversation going.
- **Create Opportunities for Team Collaboration**: Collaboration isn't just a buzzword—it's an essential leadership practice. Regularly create opportunities for your team to collaborate on projects, share best practices, and brainstorm solutions. This strengthens relationships and fosters creativity and a collective sense of ownership over the school's success.
- **Reflect on Your Leadership Impact**: Take weekly time to reflect on your leadership. Ask yourself: Are my actions reinforcing trust? Am I creating space for open, authentic conversations? How do my personal and task-oriented relationships reflect the values I want my school to represent? This ongoing reflection will help you remain intentional about your leadership and its impact.

CHAPTER FIVE
Communicate to Connect

In the late 1970s, Oprah Winfrey was told she didn't have what it took to make it in the news world. The bosses at WJZ in Baltimore said she was the "wrong color," "the wrong size," and "showed too much emotion." Talk about crushing feedback, right? But guess what? That "too much emotion" became her secret weapon—her emotional sensitivity became her superpower. Instead of trying to fit herself into their mold, Oprah leaned into her authenticity. She wasn't just aware of her emotions; she used them to connect deeply with people.

Here's the kicker: Oprah wasn't just communicating—she was connecting. Think about it. Her interviews weren't just Q&As; they were full-on conversations that made people feel seen, heard, and understood. And that's the heart of what we, as leaders, need to do. It's not enough to tell people what to do—we must build those authentic connections.

For Oprah, that shift came when she was demoted to co-host of *People Are Talking*—a show that set her up for success. She realized that success didn't come from fitting into someone else's box but from connecting with people, leading with empathy, and letting vulnerability in. One of her most pivotal interviews was with Tom Carvel, the guy behind soft-serve ice cream. Oprah said she felt "lit up from the inside" during the conversation, and from that moment, she knew: this wasn't about fitting in, it was about connecting.

Oprah's genius was her ability to connect with people on a level that made them feel valued, respected, and understood. Just like Oprah used relational intelligence to connect with her audience, great school leaders do the same with their teams. The best leaders don't just deliver information—they engage, inspire, and build trust through authentic connection.

As school leaders, our work is no different. We don't just need to communicate—we need to connect. The leaders who make a difference aren't just throwing out directions. They're bridging the gap between what's required and what's heard, between the task at hand and the emotional side of leadership. We're building relationships with our teams, allowing us to inspire and empower.

How Often Does Your Message Truly Connect?

Let's get real. As a school leader, you're juggling a lot. Between meetings, emails, tough conversations, and strategy sessions, communication can start to feel like just another item on the to-do list. But the truth is, communication is everything. And not just talking—it's about truly connecting with your team.

Ever had a moment in a meeting where you say something important, only to be met with blank stares, as if your team is hearing it for the first time? Or when you're giving a pep talk, does it feel like your words are bouncing off the walls instead of sinking in?

> Communication is everything. And not just talking—it's about truly connecting with your team.

We've all been there. And it's frustrating. But the problem isn't just *what* you say—it's *how* you say it. You deliver an inspiring talk, yet no one seems engaged. You share a powerful message, but it doesn't land. The secret to actual impact? It's not more words—it's *relational communication*.

Take a step back and think about Oprah. When she spoke to her guests, she didn't just ask questions—she created moments of real connection. That's what we need to do, too. Are you listening to what your team needs to hear, not just what you want to say? Are you making your team feel heard and understood?

It's time to dig into Relational Intelligence. It's not just about telling people what's coming next or what they need to do. It's about speaking to the heart. It's about creating a culture where everyone feels seen, respected, and part of something bigger than themselves.

The Shift: From Transactional to Relational Communication

Here's the deal: If leadership communication is purely transactional—giving orders, managing logistics, and providing feedback—you may check off tasks, but you're not building a culture of trust, engagement, and motivation. Research shows effective leaders communicate in ways that foster connection, not just compliance.

A study by *Zenger and Folkman (2020)* found that leaders who prioritize relational communication—listening, engaging in dialogue, and showing empathy—are significantly more effective at building high-performing teams. Employees are more likely to trust, collaborate, and stay engaged when they feel heard and valued.

Transactional vs. Relational Communication

Transactional Communication	Relational Communication
Focuses on delivering information	Focuses on building trust and engagement
One-way: tells people what to do	Two-way: invites discussion and input
Directive: "This is the new policy."	Collaborative: "Here's why this matters. What do you think?"
Primarily about efficiency and compliance	Primarily about connection and commitment
Can feel impersonal or routine	Creates a sense of belonging and purpose

As you can see in the chart, the core difference between transactional and relational communication lies in the *quality* of the exchange. Transactional communication tends to be more directive and efficiency-driven, whereas relational communication prioritizes dialogue, understanding, and connection.

When you shift from transactional to relational communication, you move beyond simply getting things done—you foster a culture where people are invested in the vision, not just following orders. Instead of talking *to* your team, you start communicating *with* them. That's the difference between a workplace where employees comply and one where they care.

The Heart of Relational Communication

Relational communication is all about making people feel like they matter—not just in big meetings but in day-to-day moments. It's about actively listening, understanding where others are coming from, and fostering an environment where people feel safe sharing their thoughts and ideas.

So, how do you start putting relational communication into practice?

- **Start with Curiosity**: Ask questions that show you genuinely care about the other person's perspective. "How do you feel about this?" or "What's your take on where we're heading?" These questions open up the conversation and show that you value their thoughts.
- **Use Affirming Language**: Tell them you're listening when people speak up. A simple "I appreciate your insight" or "That's a great idea—let's explore it further" makes people feel heard and valued.
- **Mind Your Body Language**: Words are powerful, but nonverbal cues matter, too. Eye contact, a smile, and even how you stand can make all the difference in how your message is received.

The Importance of Listening to Connect

As leaders, we spend so much time talking that we often forget the power of listening. However, true leadership communication starts with listening—not just hearing words, but understanding the emotions and intent behind them.

Listening isn't passive; it's an active skill that builds trust, strengthens relationships, and creates a culture where people feel valued. Research by Zenger and Folkman (2016) found that leaders who are rated as highly effective listeners are also seen as the most effective overall. Their study emphasizes that great listeners don't just remain silent—they engage, ask thoughtful questions, and create meaningful dialogue.

How to Improve Your Listening as a Leader

- **Pause before responding** – Give yourself a few seconds to process what was said instead of jumping in immediately.
- **Ask follow-up questions** – Show you care about the details by asking, "Can you tell me more about that?"
- **Reflect back what you heard** – Saying, "So, what I hear you saying is…" helps clarify understanding and builds trust.
- **Maintain eye contact and open body language** – Your nonverbal cues signal whether you're fully engaged or just waiting for your turn to speak.
- **Resist the urge to solve problems immediately** – Sometimes, people just want to be heard, not given a solution immediately.

Effective leaders don't just communicate well—they listen well. And when people feel heard, they're far more likely to be engaged, motivated, and invested in the shared vision.

Communicating to Connect: Moving Beyond the Transactional

Traditional communication often feels like a simple back-and-forth exchange, doesn't it? We talk, they listen; they respond, we react. In transactional communication, the goal is just to get things done. It's functional but lacks the deeper connection that makes real growth and transformation possible.

But when you shift to relational communication, something changes. It's no longer just exchanging information; it's about building a bridge of trust and understanding. Relational communication is a dynamic, two-way process that fully engages both parties. It's about being present, not just for the sake of checking things off a list but for the sake of genuinely connecting with others. When you communicate relationally, you're showing up as your authentic self, listening with intent, and valuing the perspectives and feelings of others.

Think about the last time you had a conversation with your team that felt like a real exchange, not just you talking and them listening, but both of you fully engaged in meaningful dialogue. When was that? How did it feel? The difference is palpable, isn't it? That's the power of relational communication.

When you embrace this approach, you go from merely managing a team to leading one. Instead of giving orders, you invite collaboration. Instead of directing, you partner. You create an environment where ideas flow freely, everyone feels heard and valued, and collective problem-solving leads to innovative solutions.

Relational communication fosters trust. Through this trust, you create a culture of transparency and mutual respect. When people feel understood and appreciated, they're more likely to contribute their best ideas and be fully invested in the team's success. This trust-based connection is what transforms individuals into a cohesive, high-performing team.

So, how do you shift from transactional to relational communication? Start by actively listening, being present in every interaction, and showing empathy. Ask questions that invite others into the conversation. Acknowledge their contributions and validate their experiences. Doing this doesn't just strengthen relationships—it creates an environment where people thrive.

This shift isn't just a nice-to-have; it's essential for building a team culture that drives results. It's what makes a team more than just a group of individuals. It's what turns a collection of voices into a united force, working together toward a shared vision. And that's when true collaboration, innovation, and success happen.

Enhancing Your Listening Skills: A Conversation

Let's chat about something essential for us as leaders: listening. We've all heard the advice about listening, but how often do we implement it? It's not always easy, especially when our minds are juggling a thousand things, but how we listen shapes everything around us. So, let's dive into a few practical ways to enhance this skill that's so important for building real connections.

Make Time

Sometimes, the best conversations happen when we least expect them. When you're always busy, it's easy to dismiss these moments, but relational communication asks us to pause and be present. As school leaders, it's our responsibility to carve out time for our teams. We must understand that a meaningful conversation might stretch longer than anticipated—but that's okay. It's in these moments that trust and collaboration take root.

Paraphrase and Summarize

When someone speaks to you, don't just hear the words. Reflect them back. This might sound simple, but it can completely change the dynamic. Try saying, "So, what I hear you saying is…" It's a game-changer. It shows that you're not just hearing but *understanding*. And that understanding? It makes people feel valued.

Ask Follow-Up Questions

Be curious rather than rushing to the next topic or wrapping things up. Ted Lasso, the ever-optimistic coach, famously said, *"Be curious, not judgmental."* That's the essence of relational leadership. Instead of assuming you know what someone means, dig deeper. Ask clarifying questions like, *"Can you tell me more about your concerns?"* or *"What challenges are you facing that I might not be seeing?"*

Research suggests that leaders who ask follow-up questions foster stronger team engagement and psychological safety (Edmondson, 2019). When people feel heard, they're more likely to trust leadership, contribute ideas, and collaborate effectively. Follow-up questions don't just clarify information—they create a culture where every voice matters.

Eliminate Distractions

This is one of the easiest things to overlook. When someone's talking, put away distractions. It's a small but powerful gesture that tells the other person, "You matter to me." Doing this creates space for the conversation that builds relationships, trust, and respect.

Now, think back to the leaders you've admired most—those who made a difference. I'll bet they weren't the loudest in the room. They took the time to listen, not just to respond, but to understand where people came from. They didn't just give advice—they empathized, they connected, and that's why people trusted them.

Listening to Yourself

As much as we talk about listening to others, listening to yourself is just as important. Do you hear people with empathy? Or are you waiting for your turn to speak? How we listen—genuinely, with care—speaks volumes about how we lead. When we listen well, our relationships thrive. And those relationships? They're the heart of outstanding leadership.

Miscommunication Among Teammates: A Personal Story

Let me share something that has stuck with me for years. A while ago, I witnessed a disagreement between two teachers. What started as a difference in opinion about a social studies lesson quickly escalated into a full-blown personal conflict. One believed in high expectations; the other thought we were setting students up for failure. The tension was thick. It would have impacted the entire team if we hadn't addressed it.

But here's what I learned: The real key wasn't in solving the disagreement but shifting their focus. I created a safe space to talk, where both voices could be heard without judgment. I reminded them that their passion for our students was why they were in this profession. We focused on the problem, not each other, and suddenly, we talked about how to make the lesson rigorous *and* accessible. Not just who was right, but how we could work together to do what was best for the students.

> When we shift from proving a point to finding solutions, we turn conflict into collaboration.

I didn't say, "You're being too harsh" or "You're too lenient." Instead, I asked, "What specifically about this lesson concerns you?" That shift in language took the conversation from defensiveness to constructive problem-solving. And it worked. They collaborated, devised a new plan, and later became an example of teamwork for the rest of the staff.

But it didn't stop there. It took time to rebuild their relationship. Over the next weeks, we checked in, and by the next semester, they were not only working well together but also modeling collaboration for everyone else. This experience taught me a crucial leadership lesson: Miscommunication isn't just about words—it's about trust. When we shift from proving a point to finding solutions, we turn conflict into collaboration. This makes the leadership insight clearer.

Creating a Culture of Connection

Building a culture of connection within your team takes intentional effort, but the rewards are immeasurable. Connection isn't built through emails or formal meetings; it's nurtured through everyday, meaningful actions. Here are a few ways to make that happen:

- **Reverse Mentoring**: Empower newer staff to share fresh insights on technology and teaching strategies with experienced leaders. This creates a two-way exchange that breaks down hierarchies and fosters a culture of mutual learning.
- **Walking Meetings**: Take meetings outside the office to reduce stress, spark creativity, and make conversations more organic. It encourages open dialogue and helps team members feel more at ease.
- **Open-Door Leadership Hours**: Set aside time each week where staff can stop by for casual, agenda-free chats. These informal interactions build trust, promote approachability, and show your team that their input matters.

The Power of Relational Communication in Times of Crisis

We all know that communication can be easy when things are calm. But when a crisis hits, that's when the true test of leadership comes in. People don't need cold directives in those moments—they need to feel connected, seen, and heard. They need to know you're there with them, guiding them through the storm.

I'll never forget the day a tornado warning occurred at our school. Amid chaos, I didn't just lead through instructions—I led with empathy. I communicated openly with my staff, reassured them, and listened to their concerns. The way I communicated in those moments became a lifeline. And it wasn't just about managing the logistics; it was about ensuring people felt supported.

In that moment, I realized that crisis leadership isn't just about control—it's about connection. When leaders communicate with transparency, calm, and care, they don't just manage emergencies—they build long-term trust. People remember how you made them feel during the most uncertain times. Relational communication in crisis doesn't just help us weather the storm; it strengthens the foundation for future challenges.

When we lead with relational communication during crises, we don't just survive the storm. We grow from it together, becoming a more resilient, unified team. These experiences teach us that trust, empathy, and clear communication are the pillars of strong leadership—not just in times of calm but especially when the storm is at its worst.

Tips for Leading with Relational Communication During a Crisis

1. **Stay Calm, Stay Grounded**: In chaos, be the calm. Your tone will set the mood for the entire team.
2. **Open the Lines for Honest Dialogue**: Create space for vulnerability. Let people share their concerns and emotions freely.
3. **Acknowledge Emotions, Reinforce Hope**: Recognize the challenges, but always remind your team of their strength and your belief in them.

Communicating with Parents: Connection Through Conflict

However, not every crisis comes from weather alerts or emergency protocols.

Sometimes, the most intense "storms" a school leader faces come from emotional, high-stakes conversations with parents. These moments may not make the evening news, but they can shape the culture of your school just as profoundly.

Whether it's a disciplinary decision, an academic concern, or a misunderstanding, how we communicate with parents during conflict sets the tone for trust, collaboration, and partnership. It's easy to become defensive or default to policies, but parents want to feel heard, understood, and assured that their child matters.

In these moments, relational communication isn't just helpful—it's vital.

But here's the leadership balance that matters most: **You must listen to parents while standing behind your teachers.** That doesn't mean dismissing a parent's concern—it means communicating with empathy while reinforcing your trust and confidence in your staff.

When leaders fail to support their teachers in front of parents, it sends a powerful message to the entire team: *You're on your own.* But when teachers know their leader will back them, even in challenging conversations, they feel empowered, trusted, and more willing to grow from feedback.

How to Navigate Difficult Conversations with Parents:

- **Start with empathy, not explanation**: "I can see how concerned you are, and I want you to know that we care deeply about your child's success."

- **Listen more than you speak**: Let parents share their thoughts fully before responding.
- **Seek to understand, not defend**: Ask, "Help me understand what you're seeing at home," instead of launching into justification.
- **Keep the student at the center**: Use language that positions you as allies: "What can we do together to support your child?"
- **Support your teachers, respectfully**: Say, "I know how committed this teacher is to your child's success. Let's work together to find a solution that supports both of you."
- **Follow up**: After a tough conversation, a quick call or email can rebuild trust and show parents you value the relationship.

When leaders communicate with relational intelligence—especially during challenging parent conversations—they build bridges between school and home and send a clear message to their staff: *I've got your back, and I trust your professionalism.*

Conclusion: Communication as Connection

Relational communication is more than just a method of exchanging information—it is the cornerstone of effective leadership and the key to cultivating a thriving, cohesive team. Authentic leadership isn't about managing tasks or directing people through the mechanics of a goal; it's about establishing connections that transcend transactional conversations and move into the realm of understanding, empathy, and trust.

Leaders who embrace relational communication create an environment where individuals don't just do their jobs—they feel valued, heard, and empowered to contribute to the collective vision. These leaders understand that their actions and words have the power to build or break relationships, and they choose to prioritize connection over control. By listening actively, showing empathy, and creating spaces for open dialogue, they foster an organizational culture where collaboration and innovation can thrive.

Relational communication becomes even more critical in challenging times, such as crises. During these moments, a leader's ability to communicate with empathy, transparency, and vulnerability can provide stability and hope. How leaders communicate in times of uncertainty shapes the resilience and unity of their teams long after the storm has passed.

Ultimately, relational communication isn't just an aspect of leadership—it's its foundation. Every interaction with your team is an opportunity to build trust, foster collaboration, and inspire growth. Leaders who invest in relational communication don't just aim for a culture of connection—they create one. So, here's the challenge: Will you lead with empathy and intention, making every conversation count? The future of your team's success depends on it.

Best Practices for Exceptional Leaders:

1. **Set Aside Time to Be in Classrooms and Interact with Staff**: Great leaders prioritize being present and engaged in classrooms. Whether an instructional leader or a teacher-leader, spending time in the classroom allows you to build strong relationships with staff and students and gain insight into their challenges and successes. It also shows your team that you are invested in their work and learning.

2. **Make Time for Relationships**: Building strong, authentic relationships is key to leadership success. Dedicate time to connect with colleagues, staff, and students. Whether through informal check-ins, team-building activities, or just offering a listening ear, making time for relationships helps foster trust and a supportive school culture that drives success.

3. **Encourage Ongoing Professional Growth**: Regardless of your role, encourage continuous development for yourself and your team. Provide opportunities for professional learning, collaboration, and mentorship. Empowering staff and students to pursue growth helps create a culture of improvement, where everyone is motivated to succeed and contribute to the school's overall success.

CHAPTER SIX
The Power of Praise: Fueling a Culture of Recognition

High engagement can't exist with low morale.

As we dive into praise, I want to start with a story. Early in my career as an administrator, I received a note from a teacher after the first week of school. It wasn't from someone expecting a big accolade or grand recognition. Instead, it came from a teacher who simply appreciated how I took the time to acknowledge even the smallest staff accomplishments. On that note, the teacher shared how hearing their name mentioned for their contributions made them feel valued, not just as a teacher, but as a person. It was a simple yet powerful moment of connection that has stayed with me throughout my career. I keep that note in my desk drawer, reminding me that praise is not just something nice to do; it's an essential part of building relationships and a positive school culture. That note reminded me of a fundamental truth: Praise isn't just about making people feel good—it's about building a culture where recognition fuels motivation, engagement, and trust. In this chapter, we'll explore how intentional praise can transform school culture, drive engagement, and elevate performance at every level.

> It's easy to get lost in the day-to-day tasks, but taking a moment to recognize even the smallest efforts can have a massive impact on the energy and morale of your team.

So, let's talk about it: How does praise shape the culture in your school? How do you use recognition to ignite motivation and create that atmosphere where people feel seen, heard, and appreciated? It's easy to get lost in the day-to-day tasks, but taking a moment to recognize even the smallest efforts can have a massive impact on the energy and morale of your team.

This brings me to the "Post-its of Praise" idea—something simple but incredibly effective. It's a term I coined to describe a practice that involves visiting classrooms and leaving behind a small note of praise. When you leave a classroom, leave a post-it with a message like, "I love how you connect with your students," or "You are so inspiring—your students are lucky to have you." These little notes, much like the ones teachers receive from students, are often kept as cherished reminders of their positive impact. I can't tell you how frequently I saw those notes displayed on the wall or pinned to the filing cabinet beside their desk. They were treasured reminders that I appreciate and see their amazing work. It's about recognizing the small wins that often go unnoticed and ensuring people feel celebrated.

Whether it's a quick note for a teacher's creative lesson plan or a student's growth, those moments of recognition create a ripple effect. What would it look like if every teacher and every leader took a minute each day to jot down a note of praise?

And here's the twist: Praise, rooted in relational intelligence, becomes more than just a "good job" or a passing compliment. Relational intelligence is about connecting with others on a deeper level, building trust, and fostering positive interactions. When we offer praise with relational intelligence, it's more personal. It says, "I see you. I hear you. Your contribution matters." It's about validating the effort, the challenges overcome, and the growth achieved—not just the outcomes.

Now, I want to flip this conversation over to you. How do you incorporate relational intelligence into your recognition efforts? Have you noticed how different people respond to various types of praise? Some might love a public shout-out in a staff meeting, while others prefer a quiet note on their desk. Praise isn't a one-size-fits-all; it's about meeting people where they are and making them feel valued in a way that resonates with them.

Praise doesn't just build morale—it builds connection. It helps us create a culture of collaboration, trust, and belonging. When we praise others thoughtfully, we're doing more than just celebrating success—we're strengthening the bond that makes everyone feel part of something bigger than themselves.

And that's where the HOPE framework comes in. While praise is a crucial piece of the puzzle, it's even more powerful when embedded within a larger support and motivation system. Have you ever considered how praise fits within a broader approach to leadership? This is where the HOPE framework—Hope, Opportunity, Praise, and Encouragement—becomes key. It's not just about recognition in isolation; it's about creating a comprehensive environment where everyone feels seen, supported, and encouraged. By integrating praise into this framework, we create a culture that acknowledges success and actively nurtures growth and development at every level.

The HOPE Framework: Building a Culture of Success through Hope, Opportunity, Praise, and Encouragement

As leaders in education, we hold the key to unlocking the potential in those we serve—whether it's our staff, students, or the broader school community. However, as leaders, we often focus on the negatives. Not because we intend to, but because our brains are wired for it. We naturally tend to seek out what might harm us—it's a survival instinct. Since this negativity bias is built into us, we tend to look for problems, and unsurprisingly, we often find exactly what we're looking for (Baumeister et al., 2001).

The danger of this mindset is that it can shape our leadership in ways we don't even realize. When we focus too much on deficits—what's missing, what's broken, what needs fixing—we risk overlooking the incredible strengths, talents, and progress around us. This kind of leadership can create a culture of fear, where staff and students feel more pressure to avoid mistakes than to strive for excellence. The HOPE framework is designed to help us reframe this tendency. It shifts our focus toward the positive, training us to look for the good in our schools, staff, and students.

Research shows that individuals need five times more praise than criticism to thrive (Losada & Heaphy, 2004). When we prioritize recognition and encouragement, we empower those around us and build a thriving environment where success becomes inevitable. This framework isn't just about being positive—it's about intentionally shaping a culture that uplifts and sustains growth. Leadership is not just about finding solutions to problems; it's about cultivating a vision that inspires, motivates, and brings out the best in everyone.

Hope

Hope is the foundation of everything. Without hope, where are we? As leaders, we're responsible for instilling hope in our staff and students. We show them that success isn't just a far-off dream—it's within reach. And how do we do that? Through praise. Whenever we recognize someone's effort, we reinforce their belief in themselves and the school's success. Praise is the spark that ignites hope.

Tip: A powerful way to promote hope is by creating small, achievable goals and celebrating progress. Hope becomes tangible when staff and students can see the steps toward success. Keep celebrating the small wins—it builds momentum!

Opportunity

Next comes Opportunity. We grow by trying new things, taking risks, and challenging ourselves. Praise plays a big role here, too. When you acknowledge someone's effort to try something new—an innovative lesson plan or a new teaching strategy—you're not just saying, *"Good job."* You're creating an opportunity for them to grow, learn, and continue improving. When students see that their efforts, no matter how small, are noticed, they begin to believe that they, too, have the opportunity for success.

Tip: Provide opportunities for peer collaboration and professional development. Offering staff opportunities to innovate and take risks within a supportive environment can make a huge difference in cultivating opportunity.

Praise

Now, praise—this is the glue that holds everything together. It's not just a one-time acknowledgment of a big win. Praise has to be consistent, sincere, and meaningful. Research (Losada & Heaphy, 2004) has shown that individuals need five positive affirmations for every piece of criticism to maintain motivation and self-esteem. This 5:1 praise-to-criticism ratio, identified in studies on workplace and educational psychology, underscores the need to shift our approach from the traditional praise-criticism-praise sandwich, which can dilute the impact of praise and feedback.

The "sandwich" approach, commonly used in teacher evaluations, cushions negative feedback between two layers of positive comments. While leaders often default to this technique to soften the impact of criticism, it can end up feeling transactional and insincere. Instead of using praise as a buffer to smooth over the criticism, it's more effective to make praise a sincere and focused expression of recognition. When praise is genuine and directly tied to specific actions, it becomes a meaningful part of the feedback process, not just a technique to "soften the blow."

Critiquing is essential for growth, but when feedback is delivered through a formulaic structure, the positive reinforcement can lose its impact. People disengage if they feel the praise is merely a transactional buffer rather than an authentic acknowledgment of their contributions.

Instead of relying on the praise-criticism-praise model, we should prioritize consistent, meaningful praise and feedback centered around strengths, effort, and improvement. This approach strengthens relationships, fuels motivation, and builds a culture of trust. People perform their best when they feel seen, valued, and encouraged—not because they fear criticism, but because they are empowered to grow and improve.

Tip: Make praise a routine. Ensure praise flows regularly during a staff meeting or a casual encounter in the hallway. Make it a part of your school's daily language—"Thank you for your patience," "I see how much effort you're putting into this project." By embedding praise into the fabric of your school culture, you foster a space where people feel encouraged to do their best, knowing their contributions are valued.

Encouragement

And finally, Encouragement. This one's huge, isn't it? Praise acknowledges achievement, but encouragement fuels the fire to keep going. It's about telling someone, *"I believe in you. You've got this,"* even when the road gets tough. It's about seeing potential in someone, not just their past performance. Encouragement keeps people pushing forward, motivated to grow, and contributing to the whole team's success.

Tip: Encourage growth by emphasizing effort over perfection. Highlight moments where perseverance paid off, showing that growth comes from continuous effort, not immediate success.

Wrap-Up: Why the HOPE Framework Matters

Integrating Hope, Opportunity, Praise, and Encouragement into our everyday leadership practices isn't just a feel-good gesture; it's a transformative strategy that directly impacts the success of our staff and students. When we actively foster an environment where hope is cultivated, opportunities are created, praise is frequent, and encouragement is given, we build a thriving school culture.

These elements are not just *"nice-to-haves"* but essential in empowering people to be their best selves. By nurturing these qualities, we equip others with the belief in their abilities, the support to take risks, and the motivation to keep pushing toward success. As leaders, it's our responsibility to model and champion these values daily, ensuring that everyone in our school community feels seen, valued, and ready to reach their fullest potential.

Let's create a culture of hope and achievement, one small action at a time.

Encouraging Peer-to-Peer Praise

One of the most powerful ways to recognize and boost school morale is by encouraging **peer-to-peer praise**. Sure, recognition from administrators is key, but let's be honest—staff members often feel more connected to their colleagues than the leadership team. When your peers show you appreciation, it means something special. So, empowering your staff to give each other shout-outs makes them feel valued and helps foster a positive and collaborative environment.

As an administrator, you're the one who sets the tone for this culture. Don't just wait for big moments—encourage your team to shout each other out for the small wins too. Whether it's a creative lesson plan, stepping in to help during a tough moment, or offering emotional support when someone's going through a hard time, these little acts of recognition can make a huge impact. It could be as simple as a handwritten note, a comment in a meeting, or a shout-out in the staff group chat. The more staff members feel appreciated by one another, the stronger the bond and sense of belonging within the school community.

Tip: Consider creating informal "shout-out" rituals, like dedicating a small portion of every staff meeting for peer recognition. Acknowledge a colleague's effort every time you meet as a team.

Creating and Sustaining a Culture of Appreciation

When I first became a school leader, one thing stood out: while our team was incredibly hardworking, there wasn't much recognition between staff members. We knew we were working hard, but the effort didn't always feel acknowledged. I wanted to create an environment where everyone felt appreciated, so we made the "Staff Shout Out Wall."

The idea was simple but powerful. We turned a prominent wall in the copy room into a space for teachers, administrators, support staff, and paraeducators to post handwritten notes praising their colleagues. Each month, every staff member got a bundle of these notes delivered to their mailbox. To keep things fun, we made it a bit of a contest—anyone who contributed a note got entered into a drawing for a coffee and donut from a local breakfast spot.

At first, the wall was a bit quiet. But after a few weeks, it started to fill up with colorful messages of gratitude—"Thanks for helping me out in class today!" or "I appreciate you stepping in for me during that meeting!" Walking by the wall daily made me smile, seeing all these personal notes. It became more than just a bulletin board—a vibrant representation of our school's values.

One of my favorite moments was when a very reserved art teacher, known for her quiet dedication, received a note from a paraeducator who worked with her. The note praised how the art teacher had handled a difficult situation with a student struggling with behavior. It was an incredibly thoughtful and specific recognition of her patience, empathy, and the positive impact on the student and the entire classroom. When the art teacher received her bundle of notes that month, I remember seeing her read them quietly with a soft smile. It meant so much to her—more than any public accolade could have.

Over time, the Staff Shout Out Wall became more than just a place to post compliments—it became a catalyst for change. Staff started sharing ideas more openly. The culture of appreciation spread beyond the walls, and it was like a domino effect. Teachers were more willing to collaborate, share best practices, and openly support each other. The small act of recognition had a lasting impact, and it became one of the core values that defined our school.

The Game-Changer: The Power of Feeling Valued

Here's a truth bomb: When teachers feel valued, they're six times more engaged. That's right—six times. This isn't just a number on a chart; it's a game-changer for your whole school culture. Now, let's break that down a bit. Research shows that 70% of teachers don't feel valued by their leaders. That's a huge issue because when teachers don't feel appreciated, it leads to disengagement, burnout, and—let's face it—a toxic culture.

I was reminded of just how critical feeling valued is when a teacher approached me after one of my keynotes. She shared her frustration with me, saying, *"I teach science and put together this amazing project for my students. I wanted to showcase it to the school. No administrator ever came by to see it, nor did anyone acknowledge it. It was like it never happened, like I didn't even exist. Do you think I feel valued, or will I ever try something like that again?"*

Her words were powerful. This teacher had invested her time, effort, and passion into something she believed in, but she felt invisible and unappreciated because no one acknowledged her work. And that's the sad reality for so many teachers. When they don't feel valued, their engagement plummets.

Six Times More Engagement—What It Means

Being six times more engaged doesn't mean just showing up for work—it means being all in. It's a radical shift in the way teachers approach their jobs. But when teachers don't feel valued, the opposite happens: they disengage. They stop giving that extra effort because they think their contributions aren't seen or acknowledged.

Reflecting on that teacher's story, I see why many teachers struggle to stay engaged. They put in the hard work, but it's hard to stay motivated when no one recognizes it. Research (Gallup, 2017) shows that teachers who don't feel valued by their leaders aren't just disengaged—they often lose the drive to try anything new or innovative again.

But when teachers do feel valued, everything changes. Their teaching, relationships with students, and contributions to the school all transform.

Teachers who feel appreciated don't just work harder—they teach better. Engaged teachers create engaged classrooms. They experiment with new teaching methods, collaborate more with colleagues, and foster student-centered learning environments that drive academic success. Recognizing teachers isn't just about making them feel good—it's about creating a ripple effect that transforms the entire school culture. When teachers feel valued, students feel the impact: higher engagement, better learning outcomes, and an environment where growth and collaboration thrive.

> Engaged teachers create
> engaged classrooms.

Why Feeling Valued is a Game-Changer

The gap between an engaged teacher and one who feels overlooked or undervalued is massive. Engaged teachers become agents of change in their classrooms and the school culture. Teachers who feel appreciated are likelier to invest in their students' success, innovate in the classroom, and collaborate with their peers.

In that teacher's case, if she had been acknowledged, her passion for the project could have spread to others. Instead, her disappointment and lack of recognition created disengagement, and in all likelihood, she won't put that kind of effort into another project again. Teachers need to know their efforts matter—it's that simple. Valued teachers do more than just teach—they create a ripple effect throughout the school.

Here's how:

- **Higher Teacher Engagement = Higher Student Success**: Engaged teachers are invested in their students' success. They customize their teaching to ensure every student gets the attention they need, which leads to better outcomes for everyone.
- **Stronger Collaboration and Innovation**: Teachers who feel valued aren't just focused on their classrooms—they share ideas, collaborate with their peers, and drive innovation across the school.
- **Teacher Resilience**: When teachers feel appreciated, they can handle challenges better. They become more resilient, facing obstacles with a positive mindset and finding creative solutions. This resilience spreads, creating a positive, solution-oriented school culture.

The Domino Effect: From Teachers to Students to School Culture

The impact of feeling valued doesn't just stay within the classroom—it spreads throughout the school. When teachers feel appreciated, they give their best, and that energy inspires everyone around them.

- **Teachers Collaborate Freely**: Engaged teachers mentor one another, share resources, and tackle challenges together. It builds a culture of teamwork and innovation.
- **Students Feel the Energy**: When teachers are more engaged, students can feel that energy, too. They're motivated to learn, to ask questions, and to take ownership of their education.
- **A Unified, Thriving School Culture**: A school where teachers and students are both highly engaged creates a culture of success that touches every aspect of the school—academically, emotionally, and socially.

The Bottom Line: Six Times More Engagement Transforms Everything

When teachers feel valued, they become six times more engaged, and this isn't just a slight boost—it's a complete transformation. It leads to:

- **Higher Teacher Retention**: Research shows that teachers who feel valued by their leaders are likelier to remain in their positions. According to Gallup's State of the American Workplace report, employees who feel appreciated are significantly more likely to stay in their roles, and this holds true for teachers as well. Specifically, teachers who feel engaged and valued are less likely to leave the profession (Gallup, 2017).
- **Improved Student Outcomes:** The link between engaged teachers and improved student outcomes is well-documented. A study by Hattie (2009), which synthesized thousands of research studies, found that teacher effectiveness has a significant impact on student learning. Engaged teachers are more likely to develop innovative teaching practices and create positive student-teacher relationships, leading to better academic results (Hattie, 2009).
- **A Thriving School Culture**: A thriving school culture is directly tied to teacher engagement. According to research by the Wallace Foundation, effective school leadership creates a culture of high expectations and a supportive environment, which is essential for teachers to feel valued and for students to succeed. Teachers who are engaged and valued contribute to a culture of excellence and

collaboration, which has a positive ripple effect throughout the entire school (Leithwood, Louis, Anderson, & Wahlstrom, 2004).

In short, making teachers feel valued is not just nice—it's essential for creating a school where everyone thrives.

Avoiding Pitfalls in Praise and Recognition

To ensure your praise remains meaningful and effective, keep these best practices in mind:

- **Be Specific**: Instead of generic praise like "Great job!" get specific: "Your lesson on fractions today was so engaging—students were excited to participate."
- **Be Balanced**: Too much praise can feel routine, while too little can lead to disengagement. Find a rhythm that recognizes achievements when they're truly deserving but allows space for growth without constant reinforcement.
- **Be Fair**: Ensure recognition is spread equitably. Don't favor specific individuals—acknowledge each person's unique strengths and contributions.
- **Be Timely**: Praise is most impactful when it's immediate. Don't wait for formal evaluations to recognize great work. Acknowledge efforts right away to show you're paying attention.

Practical Ideas for Celebrating Staff and Student Achievements

Let's talk about celebrating the hard work and successes of staff and students in ways that make everyone feel valued. You've probably already used things like "Post-its of Praise" or the "Staff Shout-Out Wall," but here are a few other ideas to keep the recognition flowing and foster a culture of appreciation:

Public Recognition at Meetings

How often do you take a moment during staff meetings or assemblies to highlight a staff member's or student's achievements? It's a small gesture, but giving someone public recognition, whether for an innovative lesson or a student's progress, makes a huge impact. And it's not just about academics! Think about celebrating someone who goes above and beyond to help a colleague or a staff member who's been the quiet champion of student well-being behind the scenes. Recognition can take many forms!

Personalized Notes of Appreciation

Have you ever taken a few minutes to write a handwritten note, send an email, or even send a quick message to someone to say "thank you"? Those little gestures might seem small, but they go a long way. Imagine telling a teacher, "Your dedication to that project made a difference," or thanking a staff member for outstanding support to the team. People love to feel seen and appreciated for the unique contributions they bring to the table.

Staff Shout-Outs in Smaller Teams

How about encouraging your staff to give shout-outs within their smaller teams or grade levels? This helps create a more personal space for recognition, making everyone feel like they're part of the celebration, not just the big public moments. Plus, it avoids any sense of favoritism and ensures no one's efforts go unnoticed.

Student Recognition

Don't forget about your students! Public shout-outs for their academic or non-academic achievements during assemblies, or even just in the classroom, can boost their confidence and inspire them to keep working hard. Everyone loves to hear that their effort is noticed, right? Whether it's a perfect test score or showing kindness to others, recognition is a powerful motivator.

Take Positive Pictures to Share in Newsletters and Social Media

A picture is worth 1,000 words, and as school leaders, we are in charge of how we present our school to the public. Use your phone to take pictures of students learning across the school, excellent teaching in action, and engaging family PTA events to share in the newsletter or social media! These pictures go a long way in spreading joy and spotlighting all the wonderful people in your school community!

Finally, remember that praise is not just a tool—it's a leadership imperative. A culture of appreciation and support fosters trust, drives engagement, and boosts performance. Leaders who prioritize relationships, praise consistently, and make their staff feel valued create an environment where everyone thrives. When educators feel valued, they are six times more likely to be engaged, bringing their best efforts to the classroom, directly benefiting students. By fostering a culture of respect and recognition, you're enhancing teacher satisfaction and student outcomes.

So, here's your challenge: Make praise a consistent, intentional part of your leadership practice. Ask yourself: How will you ensure your staff feels seen, valued, and appreciated every day? Start today. Your leadership will shape a culture of success that ripples throughout your school.

Best Practices in Action

1. **Tailor Praise to Individual Preferences**: Not everyone thrives under the spotlight. Understand your staff's preferences for receiving recognition and honor them. Whether they prefer public acknowledgment or a quiet, private word of thanks, customizing your approach shows that you genuinely care about their comfort and well-being.

2. **Create a Consistent Culture of Recognition**: Make praise a regular, ongoing practice within your school. Encourage staff members to celebrate each other's achievements, creating a ripple effect of positivity and motivation. When recognition becomes a part of your school's fabric, it fosters a culture where everyone feels seen, valued, and motivated to contribute their best.

TRANSITION TO PART III
The Connection Pillar

People don't commit to ideas as much as they commit to people. Strong connections turn vision into action.

Now that we've unlocked the power of trust and communication, we're moving into the final pillar of relational intelligence: **Connection**. If trust is the foundation and communication is the bridge, connection is the result—the deep, meaningful bond that forms when trust and communication align.

Connection transforms isolated individuals into cohesive teams. It turns a group of staff members into a united community working toward a shared vision. Connection also allows leaders to go beyond their own perspective, listening to and understanding the unique needs of each team member and fostering collaboration.

> In challenging moments, the relationships you've built and the trust you've established will guide your leadership.

This section explores **specific strategies for building connected, collaborative teams**. Leadership isn't a solo endeavor; it's about uniting people with a common purpose. You'll gain practical tools for fostering teamwork, ensuring everyone feels like an integral part of the process, and leveraging your staff's unique strengths.

We'll also focus on **relational intelligence in times of crisis**—the true test of connection. In challenging moments, the relationships you've built and the trust you've established will guide your leadership. You'll discover how to manage emotions, foster team-based problem-solving, and build resilience through compassionate, transparent communication.

In the next section, we'll explore how to foster real connections with your team, create collaborative cultures, and ensure that relationships aren't just strong in stable times but resilient in moments of crisis.

As we move into the Connection Pillar, you'll gain actionable insights for leading in times of stability and adversity. By focusing on real, lasting connections, you'll leave a legacy of relational leadership beyond your tenure.

CHAPTER SEVEN
From Isolation to Collaboration

The year is 1914, and Sir Ernest Shackleton, a seasoned explorer, is leading one of the most daring expeditions in history—the Imperial Trans-Antarctic Expedition. Shackleton and his crew are attempting to cross Antarctica, but their journey hits an unexpected snag when their ship, the Endurance, gets trapped in the ice of the Weddell Sea. Now they're stuck, far from civilization, in one of the most unforgiving environments on Earth.

For nearly a year, Shackleton and his 27 men faced isolation, freezing temperatures, dwindling food supplies, and the ever-present threat of disaster. Against all odds, they survive—every single one of them. And they don't just survive—they emerge from this ordeal with their spirits intact. How? The answer lies in Shackleton's deep understanding that survival wasn't just about physical strength. It was about relational intelligence. Shackleton knew that his crew's success depended not on individual might but on how they worked together as a team. He created a culture of unity, hope, and collaboration. Even when the end was near, Shackleton kept his team engaged, giving them a sense of purpose and maintaining morale in dire circumstances.

This story isn't just an extraordinary tale of survival; it's a lesson in Relational Intelligence and leadership. Shackleton didn't just issue orders and demand performance—he built relationships, nurtured trust, and ensured everyone felt heard, valued, and supported. He could have isolated himself and his crew, focusing on individual efforts, but instead, he chose collaboration. And that choice saved their lives.

Shackleton's leadership in crisis wasn't just about survival—it was about fostering a culture where every individual felt valued, challenges were faced together, and no one was left behind. Schools may not be life-or-death situations, but they do require leaders who understand that the success of students and staff depends on collaboration, trust, and shared purpose.

As school leaders, we often face the temptation to go it alone. Whether it's the pressure of daily responsibilities or the belief that we can handle things better independently, isolation can feel like an easier path. But here's the truth: Collaboration isn't just a nice idea in education—it's a game-changer. It's the heartbeat of effective leadership, high-performing schools, and sustained student success. And if we're going to make a lasting impact, we need to shift from working alone to working together.

Creating a collaborative culture in schools doesn't happen by accident. It takes intentionality, vision, and the will to unite people around a common purpose. And when we do, the results are incredible—not just for students but for everyone involved in the educational journey. So, let's explore how we can move from isolation to collaboration and build a school environment where no one is left behind.

Building Collaborative Teams in Education: The Path to Collective Success

Imagine a school where collaboration is as essential as air—where teachers, administrators, and staff unite their unique strengths toward a shared vision. In this environment, collaboration isn't just encouraged, it's the heartbeat of success. Without it, a school is like a sports team where no one passes the ball—talent is squandered, opportunities are missed, and the game falls apart. The same goes for the classroom: without collaboration, teachers face burnout, frustration, and missed opportunities for their students.

Collaboration isn't simply about working side by side. It's about creating a culture where every individual's contribution is valued and amplified. It's where student growth is directly tied to the growth of the educators who support them. In a truly collaborative environment, everyone—students, teachers, and staff—becomes part of something greater than themselves. This collective spirit is the foundation for a sustainable, thriving school community.

To understand the power of collaboration, think of Babe Ruth's words: "The way a team plays as a whole determines its success. You may have the greatest bunch of individual stars in the world, but if they don't play together, the club won't be worth a dime." In schools, no matter how brilliant or committed individual educators are, their impact is limited when they work alone. The true power of education lies in the collective energy of a team that collaborates, challenges, and supports each other to achieve the greater goal of student success.

When educators collaborate, the magic of synergy happens. Ideas flow, challenges are faced together, and decisions are made with everyone's best interests at heart. Trust deepens, and with it comes a sense of shared responsibility. Teachers stop seeing their success as individual; they see it as collective. They feel accountable not only for their own students but also for the success of their peers.

Collaboration also builds confidence. Teachers supported by their colleagues feel empowered to take risks, try new strategies, and grow their craft. They know they aren't alone in their struggles. The shift is significant—from "I need to succeed" to "We need to succeed." This mindset fosters an environment of respect, cooperation, and shared purpose.

However, when collaboration is absent, the consequences are clear. Teachers may isolate themselves, prioritize competition over cooperation, and lose their sense of community. The school's culture weakens, and the collective impact diminishes. Without collaboration, a school is like a team of all-stars who refuse to pass the ball—no matter how talented the individuals, they can't win the game alone.

> Without collaboration, a school is like a team of all-stars who refuse to pass the ball—no matter how talented the individuals, they can't win the game alone.

High-performing schools instinctively recognize this. They actively cultivate environments where collaboration thrives—where everyone, from teachers to administrators to support staff, works together toward one shared goal: the success of their students.

Moving from Isolation to Collaboration

Shifting from isolation to collaboration doesn't happen overnight. It requires intention, patience, and sometimes, a little creativity. But when you create a culture where collaboration is the norm, you're setting the stage for extraordinary success—for your team, students, and school community. What does that look like for you? What steps can you take today to foster a more collaborative environment in your school?

It's essential to recognize that we, as leaders, hold the power to shape the culture of our teams. How might you model the behaviors you want to see? How can you inspire your colleagues to trust each other and build lasting relationships? Think of the people who have impacted you most throughout your career. What qualities did they possess that allowed you to connect and collaborate with them? How can you bring some of those qualities into your leadership practice?

Let's take a page from Shackleton's book. He was a leader who understood that a team's strength and resilience depend on deep relationships built on trust and shared purpose. Educational leaders have the same opportunity to build strong, united teams. How can you ensure that every team member feels supported and valued? Building these relationships isn't just a "nice-to-have"—the foundation for collaboration unlocks greatness.

The Power of Collective Vision and Defined Purpose

Imagine a ship's crew navigating the vast ocean. Even the most skilled sailors may find themselves adrift without a clear destination. In education, our teams of educators are much like that crew—they need a shared vision and a clear purpose to guide their collective efforts. What's your vision for your school? How do you ensure everyone, from the front office to the classroom, works toward the same goals?

Collaboration becomes beneficial and essential when educators work toward a common objective, like improving student achievement or fostering emotional well-being. Have you ever seen the magic that happens when everyone in a team is pulling in the same direction? A special energy emerges when individuals realize their efforts are part of something bigger. How can you cultivate that energy in your school?

Research shows that teams with a clear purpose are more focused and productive. But how do you ensure your team understands the "why" behind what they do? How do you connect their day-to-day tasks to a larger mission? Purpose isn't just a buzzword—it's the catalyst that ignites motivation. McKinsey & Company (2020) emphasizes that when employees align their purpose with the organization's mission, they are more productive, engaged, and committed. Purpose-driven teams experience higher levels of innovation and success. How can you reignite that spark within your team? Creating clear communication around your team's mission and regularly emphasizing how their contributions connect to larger organizational goals can keep motivation and performance strong.

One key element of a purpose-driven team is shared responsibility. When everyone feels accountable not only for their own success but also for the success of their colleagues and students, the sense of ownership and collaboration deepens. How can you encourage this sense of shared responsibility in your team? How can you model it for others?

When educators feel connected and supported, their self-efficacy increases. Do your teachers perform better when they feel confident and empowered? What strategies can you implement to ensure that every team member feels seen, valued, and capable of making a difference?

On the other hand, when collaboration is absent or poorly executed, the culture suffers. Team members may become focused on individual success or self-preservation, undermining the collective vision. How can you prevent this fragmentation from happening in your school? What actions can you take to ensure that collaboration remains a priority, even in challenging times?

Building Trust Through Collaboration

One of the most powerful ways to build trust is through collaboration. Have you ever experienced a moment where collaboration transformed a team? I'll never forget an experience at my school where collaboration truly shifted the culture. Our paraprofessionals often felt excluded from meaningful conversations, and teachers sometimes viewed them as mere assistants. Sound familiar?

To bridge this gap, we introduced a "Strengths in the Classroom" session, where teachers and paraprofessionals paired up to share what they brought to the classroom beyond their formal roles. One moment I'll never forget was when our social studies teacher discovered that her paraprofessional was fluent in Spanish and had been informally helping students with English-language skills. The teacher was stunned! This newfound understanding of each other's strengths was a game-changer. How might you help your team uncover hidden strengths?

Collaboration fosters trust, and trust makes collaboration more effective. When team members feel heard and valued, they're more likely to open up and contribute ideas. But collaboration without trust is just surface-level cooperation—it lacks vulnerability, honesty, and real engagement. If team members don't trust that their contributions will be valued or that their colleagues have their backs, they'll hold back, stay defensive, and work in isolation, even if they're sitting in the same meeting. The best leaders don't just push for collaboration; they actively build trust first.

Have you seen how this openness leads to greater creativity and problem-solving? Think about the challenges you're facing right now. What new solutions might emerge if you were to tap into the collective wisdom of your team?

Effective Collaboration: Horizontal and Vertical Teams

Collaboration doesn't only happen within grade-level teams or departments. It spans horizontally and vertically, connecting educators across grade levels and subject areas. Have you ever considered the power of collaborating across disciplines or even grade levels? Horizontal teams, like those within a grade level or content area, allow educators to share resources, strategies, and insights. But the vertical collaboration—the connection between grade levels—ensures continuity and cohesion in instruction. How can you foster better alignment between grade levels?

Think of a vertical team as a bridge that connects the beginning, middle, and end of a student's educational journey. Do you see the power in having teachers across grade levels work together to ensure students receive the skills and support they need at each stage? How could this alignment improve student success and make teachers' jobs easier?

By engaging in vertical collaboration, you break down silos and create a school-wide focus on student success. Have you noticed how collaboration in one area often spills over into others? It's like a ripple effect, where ideas and strategies shared in one team inspire change in others. How can you leverage this dynamic to create a culture of continuous improvement across your school?

Cross-Departmental Collaboration: One Story, Many Perspectives

One of my most eye-opening experiences came during a cross-departmental team meeting when I was a high school science teacher. We came together to focus on a shared concern about student attendance. At first, I didn't understand how a history teacher and a school counselor could work together on this issue because they seemed to handle completely different areas, academic performance and child well-being. As the conversation unfolded, I realized attendance was connected to both, and solving it required looking at the whole student.

I walked away from that meeting with a deeper understanding of how different perspectives can shape solutions. How could your school benefit from this kind of cross-departmental collaboration? What new perspectives emerge if you bring together educators from other areas of expertise?

As a school leader, I've carried this collaborative spirit into my leadership. Schools can often be isolated, with departments or grade levels working in silos. How do you break down those silos and create a more connected school? For me, it was about creating interdisciplinary teams that worked together to analyze data and develop strategies. The result was faster decision-making, better student outcomes, and a deeper sense of shared responsibility.

How might you encourage this same level of collaboration in your school? How can you help your staff feel connected, supported, and empowered to work together toward common goals?

The power of collaboration is undeniable. When educators come together, magic happens. How can you create more opportunities for collaboration, both horizontally and vertically? How might you ensure that every voice is heard and every team member feels valued? Think about the possibilities— and then start taking action to make them a reality.

The Power of Teamwork in Education: How Collaboration Makes Schools Stronger

We all know the saying, "Teamwork makes the dream work," right? Well, in education, that couldn't be more true. Research has shown that when schools focus on collaboration, amazing things happen. We're discussing stronger teaching, better student outcomes, and a favorable school climate overall.

One of the biggest perks of collaboration is collective problem-solving. When teachers come together, it's like a brain trust where everyone's skills and ideas merge to tackle challenges head-on. Instead of solving problems alone, they can brainstorm, exchange insights, and develop solutions from everyone's expertise.

And here's the thing: When educators collaborate, accountability increases. You're not just responsible to yourself—you're accountable to your teammates. This shared responsibility helps everyone stay motivated, committed, and focused on the ultimate goal: student success.

Collaboration also fuels professional growth. Teachers who work together often see their own teaching improve because they get to share ideas, learn new strategies, and reflect on what's working (and what isn't). According to the Learning Policy Institute, schools that have collaborative professional development programs help teachers become more effective, leading to better student results. Sounds like a win-win, right?

But collaboration doesn't stop there. Collaboration also brings consistency to the table. Educators across grade levels, subjects, and departments team up to ensure that teaching strategies, policies, and expectations align. This consistency creates a smoother, more predictable learning environment, which helps students thrive academically and emotionally.

Now, let's talk about a shift that's been happening in school leadership—moving away from the traditional top-down approach to a more collaborative style called collective leadership. This model is all about empowering educators at every level to take on leadership roles, share decision-making, and have a voice in shaping the direction of the school. When teachers are actively involved in decision-making, they feel more ownership, engagement, and connection to the school's mission. This shift is not just a trend; it's a necessary transformation for schools today. In an era of increasing teacher burnout, high turnover, and diminishing morale, collective leadership is more than a good idea—it's an urgent need.

Research backs this up, too. Studies show that high-performing schools are those where teachers, administrators, and everyone involved work as a team, and decisions are made with input from various perspectives. For instance, a study from the Center for American Progress (2015) highlighted that schools with a shared leadership model, where teachers have a role in decision-making, consistently report higher levels of teacher satisfaction, retention, and student outcomes. Schools that encourage teacher leadership—whether through formal roles or informal opportunities—have more dynamic and responsive environments. Teachers can step up and lead initiatives, contribute to curriculum planning, and have a say in school policies.

But here's the kicker: Collective leadership also helps keep teachers around. When teachers feel valued and trusted in leadership roles, they're more likely to stay and feel satisfied with their careers. A study by the National Commission on Teaching and America's Future (2012) found that providing teachers with leadership opportunities helps reduce burnout and attrition. When teachers share responsibilities, the workload becomes more manageable, which helps them avoid feeling overwhelmed and undervalued.

Imagine a school where teachers feel supported, trusted, and empowered. That's a school where people stay, grow, and help each other. Collaboration and collective leadership aren't just buzzwords—they're the key to reducing burnout, improving job satisfaction, and building a thriving school community.

A Real-World Example: How Collaboration Turned a Challenge Around

Not too long ago, my team and I were dealing with a student who had some serious behavioral challenges. We could all see the stress on the teachers' faces before our meeting even started. This student was having unpredictable outbursts—sometimes shouting and throwing things. The teachers were drained, and understandably so. Not only were they worried about their safety, but also about the safety of the other students.

As the principal, I knew my role wasn't to have all the answers. I had learned early on that leadership isn't about doing everything yourself. It's about knowing how to tap into your team's strengths. This was one of those times when I needed my team just as much as they needed me.

The department lead stepped up at the meeting with her usual calm confidence. She said, "We all care about him and want the best for him, but what we've been doing isn't working. Let's rethink our approach—together."

She brought together everyone who worked with the student—his homeroom teacher, the special ed coordinator, the school counselor, the paraeducator, and the PE teacher. Each person brought a unique perspective on what triggered his behavior, what helped him, and where he struggled. Together, we pieced a clearer picture of what was going on. It wasn't random—it was about the moments when he felt unsure or embarrassed, like when transitions between activities were too sudden or when the expectations were unclear.

Once we understood the student's triggers, the team brainstormed targeted solutions. We decided to give him more advanced notice before transitions, use non-verbal cues to redirect him, and set up a quiet space where he could go to self-regulate before things escalated. One of the teachers even suggested using a discreet signal to check in with him when signs of frustration appeared.

By the end of the meeting, the team felt hopeful. Each person had contributed, and we all felt invested in the plan. We didn't just come up with solutions—we built them together.

And here's the best part: the student's behavior improved within the first week. The outbursts became less frequent, and he started using the quiet space independently. The teachers were amazed at how quickly things turned around.

But this wasn't just a win for the student—it was a turning point for our school's culture. After seeing the power of collective problem-solving, teachers became more proactive in seeking collaborative solutions for other challenges. Instead of struggling alone, they sought out colleagues, trusted the process, and worked together more than ever. The student's progress was just the beginning; the way we worked together changed for good. From then on, collaboration became more than just a strategy—it became part of our school's DNA.

Wrapping It Up: The Future of Collaboration

Looking ahead, the future of education is all about collaboration. Schools that embrace teamwork, collective leadership, and shared responsibility will not only survive—they will thrive. As new challenges emerge, collaboration will be the key to overcoming them. Whether adapting to new teaching methods, addressing diverse student needs, or managing the complexities of modern educational environments, the ability to work together effectively will be the differentiating factor.

When educators collaborate—when they share their knowledge, skills, and experiences and support each other—it creates a culture of growth, trust, and resilience. This collaborative mindset extends beyond the classroom to every corner of the school, from leadership teams to support staff. It's an environment where everyone, students and staff alike, has the opportunity to succeed.

But collaboration doesn't happen by chance. It requires intentionality, commitment, and a willingness to break down silos. Leaders must actively create the conditions that allow collaboration to flourish, whether through regular team meetings, fostering open communication, or providing opportunities for professional development. And it's not just about formal collaboration; it's about cultivating a culture where every voice is valued, every perspective is considered, and everyone is empowered to contribute.

So, ask yourself: Are you fostering a culture of collaboration, or are you unintentionally allowing isolation to take root? What's one step you can take this week to strengthen the collective leadership in your school?

> Ask yourself: Are you fostering a culture of collaboration, or are you unintentionally allowing isolation to take root?

Now is the time to make collaboration the heartbeat of your school. As you look to the future, ask yourself: How can you lead the way in fostering a collaborative culture? What steps can you take today to bring your team together, share ideas, solve problems collectively, and build a community that thrives on mutual support? The answers to these questions will shape the future of education, one where collaboration is not just a strategy but a way of life.

Let's take that first step together. The future of education is in our hands, and it starts with the way we work together. Let's make collaboration our foundation for success.

Best Practices for Fostering Collaboration

1. **Prioritize Collaborative Planning**
   - **What to do**: Set aside time for grade-level or subject teams to meet, share ideas, and improve instruction.
   - **Why it works**: Regular collaboration time leads to better strategies, clearer goals, and improved student outcomes.
2. **Cultivate Trust and Open Communication**
   - **What to do**: Encourage open dialogue, share challenges and solutions, and provide mentorship opportunities.
   - **Why it works**: When staff members trust each other, they work better together and create a more positive school culture.

3. **Empower Educators with Collective Leadership**
   - **What to do**: Give teachers leadership roles based on their strengths and involve them in school decision-making.
   - **Why it works**: When teachers feel empowered, they're more invested in the school's success, and collaboration flourishes.

CHAPTER EIGHT
Empowering Staff Through Their Unique Abilities

Great leadership is about unlocking the hidden potential that exists in every member of your team. Over the years, I've seen how a leader's ability to connect with staff can transform an entire school culture. Today, I want to share practical strategies that you can use as a school leader to empower your teachers to shine in natural, rewarding, and truly impactful ways. Because I believe that the sign of a great leader is to leave your people better than you found them, which means helping them realize and maximize their strengths and talents.

Middle school is a dynamic, sometimes challenging environment where students are beginning to find their voices amid the turbulence of early adolescence. Teachers in this setting do more than just deliver lessons—they guide young people through a critical phase of emotional, social, and academic growth. They're mentors, confidantes, and innovators who adapt daily to new challenges. In this context, empowering your staff isn't just a nice-to-have; it's necessary.

I still remember one conversation that profoundly shaped my approach to leadership. Early in my career as an administrator, I chatted casually with one of our dedicated teachers during a quiet moment in the staff lounge. This teacher, whom I'll refer to as Ms. Garcia, was known for her gentle authority and the calm energy she brought into her classroom. One day, over coffee, Ms. Garcia confided that she had been an avid gardener before she entered the profession. Her weekends were spent tending a small vegetable garden, a passion that brought her immense joy and a sense of balance.

As we talked, I saw an opportunity to bridge her passion with her professional life. I asked her, "Have you ever considered incorporating your love for gardening into your teaching?" I could see her eyes light up at the idea. We brainstormed possibilities: What if the school could have a garden project—a hands-on way for students to learn about nature, biology, and sustainability? What if Ms. Garcia could lead a garden club, sharing her passion and expertise with students who might not otherwise experience the joy of nurturing living things? That conversation was a turning point. Ms. Garcia eventually launched a garden initiative that enriched her lessons and became a beloved extracurricular activity.

This experience taught me a powerful lesson: When you connect a teacher's interests with professional opportunities, you're not merely assigning a task but nurturing a talent that can energize an entire community. When teachers feel their unique abilities are recognized and valued, they bring their whole selves to their work, inspiring colleagues and students.

Discovering Hidden Gems: A Personal Journey

Every teacher has a unique story—a hidden gem waiting to be discovered. In a middle school setting, where educators juggle curriculum demands, student behavior, and the complexities of adolescent development, it's easy for personal passions to be overshadowed by day-to-day challenges. That's why taking the time to learn about your teachers individually is vital.

I've always believed in the power of one-on-one conversations. It's in these moments—away from the structured environment of meetings and formal observations—that real insights emerge. I recall several instances where a brief chat revealed a teacher's secret passion or hidden talent. Whether it was a love for creative writing, an unexpected flair for drama, or—as in the case of Ms. Garcia—a deep-seated passion for gardening, these stories enriched my understanding of what each teacher brought.

By listening, you can discover what makes your teachers tick and how those interests might be woven into the fabric of their teaching. Recognizing and celebrating these hidden gems fosters a culture where every staff member feels seen, heard, and valued. Once we uncover these hidden talents, the next step is knowing how to cultivate them to align with the school's mission and enhance student learning.

Talent Scouting in the Middle School Environment

Imagine yourself as a talent scout, but instead of searching for star athletes or rising musicians, you're looking for the special qualities that make each teacher unique. In middle school, where educators must balance academic instruction with social-emotional support, teachers often harbor talents far beyond the classroom. They are natural storytellers, creative problem solvers, and innovators waiting to shine.

Consider the example of Ms. Garcia, the teacher who is passionate about gardening. In our conversation, her eyes sparkled when we discussed the possibility of creating a garden project that could serve as both an outdoor classroom and a community-building activity. By aligning her love for nature with a professional opportunity, we revitalized her teaching practice and provided students with a fresh, engaging way to connect with the natural world. This isn't just about adding another club or after-school program; it's about recognizing that every teacher's unique strengths can contribute to the larger mission of educating and inspiring young minds.

Strengths-based leadership means looking beyond the routine. It involves integrating those passions into everyday practice through innovative classroom projects, extracurricular activities, or collaborative initiatives that energize the entire staff.

Building a Culture of Empowerment: A Collaborative Effort

Empowerment isn't a one-time event—it's a continuous process of building trust, celebrating successes, and creating a safe, vulnerable space. In middle schools, where teachers face daily challenges ranging from shifting curricular demands to managing diverse classroom dynamics, fostering a culture of empowerment can have transformative effects.

One approach I've found effective is establishing regular opportunities for open dialogue. For instance, setting aside time for "Innovation Hours" can allow teachers to share new ideas, discuss experiments that didn't go as planned, and brainstorm solutions in a supportive environment. In these sessions, no idea is too small or too unconventional. They become a safe space where a commitment to learning and growth replaces the fear of failure.

I recall several teachers hesitating to try new approaches in their classrooms, worried that deviating from the norm might lead to criticism. By creating a forum where they could share successes and setbacks, I witnessed a gradual shift in mindset. Teachers began to see that every attempt, whether successful or not, was a stepping stone toward innovation. Over time, this culture of openness and experimentation boosted morale and led to creative teaching methods that resonated deeply with students.

> When teachers feel their ideas are valued, they're more willing to take risks and embrace change.

When teachers feel their ideas are valued, they're more willing to take risks and embrace change. This isn't just beneficial for individual growth—it has a ripple effect, enriching the entire school community.

Empowering Through Connection: The Magic of Personal Relationships

One of the most powerful aspects of relational intelligence is the ability to forge genuine connections. In the middle school environment, where teachers and students thrive on personal interaction, cultivating authentic relationships can lead to profound changes in motivation and performance. When teachers feel connected to their leader and one another, they're more inclined to invest in the school's vision and take creative risks.

One rainy afternoon, I noticed a teacher sitting quietly in the staff lounge, looking more subdued than usual. Sensing something was amiss, I invited her to share her thoughts. She expressed feeling overwhelmed by the rapid pace of curricular changes and the mounting pressure of standardized expectations. In that moment, I didn't offer quick fixes or immediate solutions; instead, I listened. I asked gentle questions about what aspects of her work she found most fulfilling and where she saw potential for integrating her interests into her teaching.

That conversation led to a breakthrough. We discussed how she might incorporate creative storytelling elements into her lessons—a nod to her love for literature and narrative. Over time, this simple adjustment reenergized her classroom and sparked greater student engagement. The lesson here is clear: genuine connection—built on empathy, active listening, and mutual respect—can empower teachers to harness their full potential.

The Pygmalion Effect: Raising Expectations, Raising Spirits

A well-documented phenomenon in education known as the Pygmalion Effect states that higher expectations lead to improved performance. When teachers know their leader believes in them, they begin believing in themselves. I've repeatedly seen this effect in action, and it's one of the simplest yet most profound tools in a leader's arsenal.

Take, for example, how I interacted with Ms. Garcia after our conversation about gardening. I made it a point to acknowledge her strengths in every meeting and highlight the innovative ways she integrated her passion into her teaching. Over time, I noticed a remarkable transformation—her confidence grew, and her enthusiasm became infectious. Colleagues began to see her as a source of inspiration, and soon, other teachers started exploring ways to integrate their interests into their classrooms.

Expressing high expectations isn't about offering empty praise—it's about setting a tone that signals to each teacher that you see greatness in them.

When your belief in someone is unwavering, they're more likely to take on challenges with renewed vigor. In a middle school environment, where every day brings new challenges, this belief can be the catalyst that transforms uncertainty into opportunity. With the understanding that expectations shape performance, let's explore practical ways to apply this principle in empowering staff.

Practical Strategies for Cultivating Empowerment

Now that we've explored some real-life stories and the theory behind relational leadership in a middle school context, let's delve into some concrete strategies you can implement to empower your staff.

1. Host Regular "Strengths Spotlights"

Set up monthly or bi-monthly sessions where teachers can share their unique talents and projects. These sessions can be informal—perhaps during a relaxed gathering in the teacher's lounge—or part of a dedicated staff meeting. The goal is to create an environment where teachers feel comfortable showcasing their hidden skills and passions. This practice not only helps in recognizing individual strengths but also encourages collaborative ideas across departments.

2. Implement Peer Mentorship Programs

Consider pairing teachers who have complementary strengths. For example, a teacher with a flair for creative arts might be paired with someone who excels in integrating technology into lessons. These partnerships can spark innovative ideas and provide mutual support. Peer mentorship also reinforces a sense of community, as teachers learn from and celebrate each other's successes.

3. Celebrate "Small Wins" Publicly

In the hustle and bustle of middle school life, it's easy to overlook the little victories. Whether it's a creative lesson plan that captivated a class, a successful extracurricular activity, or a breakthrough in student engagement, make it a point to recognize and celebrate these moments. A quick shout-out during a staff meeting, a note of appreciation on a bulletin board, or even an informal email can go a long way in boosting morale and reinforcing positive behaviors.

4. Create a Safe Space for Innovation

Establish an open-door policy where teachers feel comfortable experimenting with new ideas without fear of harsh criticism. Organize "innovation labs" or informal brainstorming sessions where staff can test new teaching methods, share feedback, and collectively troubleshoot challenges. When experimentation is celebrated, not penalized, you foster a culture where creativity and risk-taking are part of the everyday norm.

5. Schedule One-on-One Check-Ins

Regular, personalized check-ins can work wonders. Use these sessions to ask open-ended questions like, "What's one new idea you're excited to try?" or "What challenges are you facing, and how can I help?" These individual conversations build trust and provide invaluable insights into each teacher's strengths and areas for growth.

6. Integrate Personal Interests into Professional Development

Encourage teachers to blend their passions with their professional roles. If a teacher is passionate about gardening, as with Ms. Garcia, brainstorm ways to incorporate that interest into their curriculum or extracurricular activities. Whether starting a garden club, organizing nature walks, or integrating environmental science projects into lessons, aligning personal interests with professional tasks transforms routine work into meaningful, purpose-driven activities.

7. Promote Collaborative Goal-Setting

Involve your teachers in setting school-wide goals and initiatives. When teachers help shape the vision for the school, they become more invested in its success. Collaborative goal-setting ensures that everyone's voice is heard and that the objectives reflect the collective aspirations of the entire staff.

8. Offer Continuous Professional Growth Opportunities

Empowerment thrives on continuous learning. Organize workshops, invite guest speakers, and facilitate professional development sessions to develop staff strengths and relational intelligence. Encouraging teachers to pursue professional development helps bring fresh perspectives into the classroom and keeps the staff dynamic and engaged.

Real-World Examples: Lessons from the Field

Let's revisit real-world examples illustrating how empowering staff through their unique abilities can transform a middle school environment.

The Garden Initiative: A Lesson in Passion and Innovation

I often think back to that enlightening conversation with Ms. Garcia, the teacher whose love for gardening opened up a world of possibilities. During one quiet moment, as we shared during one of my "coffee chats," she revealed her passion for nurturing a small vegetable garden at home. Recognizing the potential for a hands-on learning experience, I asked her if she'd ever considered bringing that passion into the classroom. Her reaction was immediate and enthusiastic. We began discussing how a garden project could serve as an outdoor classroom. In this place, students could learn about biology, ecology, and sustainability while developing a respect for nature.

The project blossomed into something far greater than we had anticipated. Not only did Ms. Garcia lead a thriving garden club, but the initiative also spurred interdisciplinary projects. Teachers from different subjects collaborated to incorporate lessons on environmental science, art, and creative writing into the garden project. Students learned how to plant seeds, nurture them, and observe the life cycles of various plants, all while connecting theoretical knowledge with tangible experiences. This initiative became a cherished part of the school's culture, demonstrating how harnessing a teacher's passion can create ripple effects that benefit the entire community.

Innovative Learning Through Technology

Another example comes from a teacher who had long been interested in digital tools but was unsure how to bring that interest into her teaching. After several informal conversations, I paired her with a colleague adept at integrating technology into lessons. Together, they organized a series of workshops on using interactive whiteboards and educational apps. The transformation was remarkable. The once hesitant teacher began experimenting with multimedia presentations and interactive lessons that captivated her students. Her willingness to embrace technology elevated her teaching practice and inspired other staff members to explore new digital horizons.

Building Community Through Music and Art

In another instance, I encountered a teacher with a deep love for music. This teacher believed that music was not just a subject but a way to build community and express creativity. I encouraged her to lead sessions that combined music, art, and storytelling. The sessions quickly evolved into a collaborative project that involved students, parents, and fellow teachers. Through music and art, the project became a platform for expressing cultural diversity and fostering mutual respect. The initiative reminded everyone that when teachers are empowered to share their passions, they create vibrant spaces for creativity and connection.

Overcoming Challenges: Navigating Resistance and Uncertainty

Of course, not every effort to empower staff will be met with immediate enthusiasm. Resistance can manifest subtly—perhaps from teachers accustomed to routine or those who fear that standardized demands might sideline their interests. In a middle school setting, where change can feel particularly disruptive amidst the whirlwind of adolescent learning, approaching resistance with empathy is essential.

I've encountered situations where veteran teachers were initially reluctant to leave their comfort zones. In these cases, leading by example proved invaluable. I openly shared my experiences with trial and error, emphasizing that growth often comes from small, iterative steps rather than overnight transformations. The fear of failure gradually diminished by creating opportunities for teachers to experiment in low-stakes environments, through pilot projects, informal innovation labs, or small-group collaborations. Over time, teachers began to see that every experiment, regardless of its immediate success, contributed to a culture of learning and innovation.

Breaking Through Resistance: Overcoming Common Barriers to Empowerment

While it's important to acknowledge the resistance, knowing how to overcome it is just as crucial. Here are a few strategies that can help leaders navigate common barriers:

- **For Fear of Failure**: Normalize trial and error by celebrating "learning moments" rather than successes. Highlighting the value of learning from mistakes encourages a growth mindset and reduces the fear that failure will be punished. When teachers see failure as part of the learning process, they become more willing to take risks.

- **For Time Constraints**: Show teachers how integrating their passions doesn't have to be extra work, but can enhance and simplify their existing teaching. Encourage teachers to align their interests with curriculum goals, finding ways to integrate those passions into their lessons in a manageable way. This can make their teaching more enjoyable and sustainable, while still achieving educational objectives.
- **For Low Confidence**: Provide micro-leadership opportunities to build confidence. For example, ask a teacher to co-facilitate a small team discussion before leading a full PD session. Teachers can build their leadership skills in a supportive, non-threatening environment by starting small. These micro-leadership moments allow teachers to gain confidence without feeling overwhelmed.

It's important to remember that change is gradual. Empowerment is not about forcing a revolution in one day; it's about nurturing a mindset that welcomes continuous improvement. Every small step—a shared idea, an experimental project, a moment of genuine connection—builds toward a more significant transformation that can redefine the entire school community.

> Empowerment is not about forcing a revolution in one day; it's about nurturing a mindset that welcomes continuous improvement.

Creating a Lasting Impact: Strategies for Long-Term Success

Empowering your staff isn't a one-off project; it's a commitment to nurturing potential, celebrating individuality, and fostering a culture of continuous learning and collaboration. School leaders must embed empowerment into their culture and structure to ensure that empowerment becomes an ongoing process. Here are strategies to make empowerment a lasting part of your school's environment:

Sustaining Growth Over Time

- **Long-Term Coaching Structures**: As you empower your staff, it is important to move from informal check-ins to more structured career development pathways. Consider establishing mentorship programs, offering opportunities for teachers to transition into instructional coaching roles, and providing regular feedback sessions to ensure continued professional growth. These structures help create a clear path for teacher advancement and ensure that professional development is an ongoing, supportive process.

- **Tracking Professional Growth**: Leaders should track and revisit teachers' progress in integrating their passions and strengths into their teaching practices. Regularly revisiting individual progress helps to celebrate success and identify areas for further growth. This could involve maintaining a record of teachers' achievements, integrating personalized development goals, and ensuring that these goals align with the school's long-term vision.

- **Leadership Pipeline Creation**: Encourage teachers to step into mentorship or leadership roles as part of their professional journey. By developing a leadership pipeline, school leaders can create opportunities for teachers to take on new responsibilities, from mentoring new staff to leading professional development sessions. This gradual shift into leadership roles ensures the school's vision is continuously nurtured and carried forward by a team of empowered educators.

Additional Strategies for Lasting Empowerment

- **Develop a Leadership Pipeline**: Encourage promising teachers to take on leadership roles, such as mentoring new staff, leading professional development sessions, or spearheading innovative projects. Building a robust leadership pipeline nurtures individual growth and ensures the school's vision is sustained over time.

- **Document and Share Success Stories**: Record the initiatives that have worked well and the teachers behind them. Sharing these stories—whether during staff meetings, newsletters, or local education forums—can inspire others and build momentum for future projects. Celebrating successes creates a positive feedback loop that encourages further engagement and innovation.

- **Regularly Revisit and Revise Goals**: Schools' needs evolve rapidly. Periodically review your school's goals and teachers' roles in achieving them. Solicit honest feedback and be willing to adjust strategies as necessary. This commitment to continuous improvement demonstrates that you value your team's input and are invested in their professional growth.

- **Invest in Professional Development Focused on Relational Intelligence**: Offer workshops and training sessions that address academic subjects and soft skills such as emotional intelligence, active listening, and conflict resolution. When teachers develop these relational skills, they're better equipped to connect with students, colleagues, and the broader community.
- **Foster a Culture of Gratitude and Recognition**: Make recognition a regular part of your school's culture. Whether through formal awards, informal shout-outs during staff meetings, or simple thank-you notes, acknowledging your team's efforts reinforces their commitment and inspires continued excellence.

To cultivate a lasting culture of empowerment, school leaders must be proactive in ensuring that professional development and leadership opportunities extend beyond the initial phases of empowerment. Leaders create an environment where teachers are continuously supported, motivated, and equipped to grow by establishing long-term support structures, tracking progress, and fostering a leadership pipeline. This ongoing commitment to development ensures that empowerment isn't just a momentary spark but a sustained and transformative force within the school community.

Empowerment as a Journey, Not a Destination

Empowering your staff creates an environment where teachers feel seen, valued, and supported using their unique gifts. In the dynamic and sometimes unpredictable world, a leader who practices relational intelligence can transform the entire educational experience. Connecting personal passions with professional roles, fostering genuine relationships, and celebrating every small win lay the foundation for a school culture where empowerment isn't just an abstract idea—it's a lived, daily reality.

Think back to the garden initiative sparked by Ms. Garcia's passion, the innovative strides made through digital learning collaborations, and the community built around music and art. These aren't isolated success stories; they are living examples of what can happen when you invest in the unique strengths of your staff. When teachers feel empowered, they don't merely deliver lessons—they inspire, innovate, and create ripples that extend far beyond the classroom.

As you continue your journey as a middle school leader, ask yourself:

- How can I better recognize and nurture the hidden talents of my staff?
- What small changes can I implement today that will have a last-

ing impact on our school culture tomorrow?

- How can I create more opportunities for teachers to blend their passions with their professional roles?

Leadership is not a destination but a continuous journey—a series of deliberate, heartfelt actions that build toward lasting change. The power of relational leadership lies in transforming everyday interactions into opportunities for growth, connection, and empowerment.

Best Practices in Action: Your Role in Empowering the Future

Now is the time to put these strategies into practice. Think of yourself not merely as an administrator but as a mentor, a guide, and a collaborator. Your role is to inspire and support your teachers, helping them unlock their full potential so they, in turn, can encourage your students.

Consider these reflective questions as you move forward:

- What hidden talents might be waiting to be discovered among my staff?
- How can I create more platforms for teachers to share their passions and innovative ideas?
- What small, meaningful changes can I implement today to build a legacy of empowerment and excellence in our school community?

By embracing these questions and taking deliberate steps toward fostering empowerment, you're not just shaping the future of your school—you're laying the groundwork for a community where every teacher and every student has the opportunity to thrive. Empowerment is a daily act of leadership—one conversation, one risk, one moment of belief at a time. The schools that thrive are those where leaders commit not just to policies, but to people. As you move forward, ask yourself: What hidden brilliance might be waiting in your school right now—and what will you do today to unlock it?

When you unlock the hidden potential in your staff, you ignite a spark that can transform not only your school but also the lives of the young people you serve. Let's continue scouting for hidden talents, fostering genuine connections, and building a community where every teacher feels empowered to bring their best selves to work.

Thank you for joining me on this exploration of empowering staff through their unique abilities. As you integrate these ideas into your leadership practice, I hope you witness the remarkable transformation that occurs when teachers are given the freedom to be their authentic selves. We can create a school culture where empowerment, creativity, and collaboration are encouraged and celebrated daily.

Embrace the journey wholeheartedly, knowing the entire school shines brighter when teachers are empowered.

CHAPTER NINE
Boundaries and Balance

Education is a people-centered profession, and as leaders, we often feel the pressure to always be available to staff, students, parents, and district leaders. When every request feels urgent and every "please" seems to demand an immediate "yes," the inevitable result is exhaustion. Burnout doesn't just affect individual leaders; it ripples throughout our schools, impacting staff morale, school culture, and ultimately, the success of our students.

Setting boundaries isn't about being less committed—it's about being more intentional. When leaders protect their time and energy, they don't become less available—they become more effective, present, and deliberate in their leadership. **Boundaries aren't barriers; they are the foundation of sustainable, effective leadership.** Without them, leaders operate in survival mode, reacting to demands rather than leading with vision. And yes, sometimes that means saying no. No to unrealistic expectations. No to constantly putting others' needs ahead of your own. No to the idea that leadership means being on call 24/7. Because when you learn to say no to the right things, you're making room to say yes to what truly matters: building strong relationships, fostering a positive culture, and leading with energy and purpose.

> When leaders protect their time and energy, they don't become less available—they become more effective, present, and deliberate in their leadership.

This chapter will explore how boundaries and balance go hand in hand. We'll examine how Relational Intelligence can be a powerful tool to protect your well-being and share practical strategies for setting limits without sacrificing connection. Remember: the best leaders aren't the ones who do everything—they're the ones who know what's truly worth their time and energy.

The Human Side of Leadership: Why Boundaries Matter

Let's start with a simple truth: Leadership is inherently human. We lead because we care, and we care because we're connected. Yet, in our eagerness to serve our teams and students, we sometimes carry more than we can manage. I remember early in my career as an administrator, when I was still learning the ropes, witnessing an experience that resonates with me.

I recall a new teacher, bright-eyed and enthusiastic, who left school each day with a red flyer wagon piled high with books, curriculum guides, and every scrap of material she thought might help her in the classroom. Day after day, I watched her haul that heavy load to her car. With every trip, her energy visibly diminished. It wasn't just the physical weight—the burden of endless tasks and the pressure to do everything perfectly without help. I could see the frustration and exhaustion etched on her face. She was overwhelmed, yet she persisted, day in and day out.

One evening, as she was loading her wagon again, I couldn't stand by any longer. I walked over, gently asked if I could help, and took hold of the wagon's handle. "The world won't end," I told her. "You're not going to get fired. Whatever you need to work on, you can wait until tomorrow." At that moment, I reassured her that it was okay to set down that heavy load, to pause and catch her breath. For a brief instant, I saw a spark of relief in her eyes. It was as if a small part of that overwhelming burden had been lifted.

That evening taught me something crucial: If teachers struggle to carry their burdens alone, leaders do too. The constant pressure to be 'always on' isn't sustainable—not for educators and those leading them. Just as that teacher needed permission to pause, leaders must permit themselves to set boundaries.

Boundaries and Relational Intelligence: Connecting with Clarity and Purpose

Relational Intelligence is the ability to connect deeply with others while maintaining a strong sense of self-awareness. It's about balancing empathy with healthy self-care. And here's the secret: boundaries are the foundation upon which relational intelligence is built.

Imagine trying to have a meaningful conversation in a noisy, crowded room. It becomes impossible to connect without clear boundaries and lines that separate what is and isn't acceptable noise. The same idea applies in leadership. Without boundaries, trust erodes, resentment builds, and burnout becomes almost inevitable.

Think about a constantly overwhelmed leader who responds to every email at midnight, takes on every request, and never says no. Over time, they aren't more effective; they're more exhausted. Their communication becomes reactive rather than strategic. Their relationships suffer because they are too drained to be fully present. **Leaders with weak boundaries often struggle**

with relational intelligence in very tangible ways. They find themselves constantly pulled in different directions, reacting to the loudest voices rather than leading with intention. They overextend themselves, making commitments they can't sustain, leading to their team's frustration when they fail to follow through. In trying to be available to everyone, they become emotionally drained, leaving little energy for meaningful, strategic connections.

On the other hand, leaders with high relational intelligence recognize that setting boundaries isn't about detachment—it's about leading with clarity, intention, and presence. They understand that boundaries are not barriers but the framework that allows sustainable, deep connections to flourish. Here's what that looks like in practice:

- **Protecting Energy and Mental Clarity**: By setting limits on when and how you engage, you ensure you are fully present for meaningful interactions. Your energy remains intact, allowing you to think clearly and act decisively.
- **Fostering Mutual Respect**: When you communicate clear expectations—for yourself and those around you—you create an environment where mutual respect is the norm. People appreciate knowing what to expect, and it cultivates a culture of trust.
- **Modeling a Healthy Work-Life Balance**: Honoring your limits sends your staff and students a powerful message. You demonstrate that taking care of oneself is not only acceptable but essential.
- **Improving Decision-Making**: With boundaries in place, you're less likely to make reactive choices driven by exhaustion or obligation. Instead, you create space for thoughtful decision-making and strategic leadership.

In this light, boundaries are not walls designed to keep people out. Instead, they are the scaffolding that supports strong, authentic relationships. When you protect your energy, you can better connect with others on a deeper level because you're not running on empty. In other words, by taking care of yourself first, you're saying "yes" to deeper connections, improved decision-making, and sustainable leadership.

> The more we allow digital demands to dictate our day, the less mental space we have for the deep thinking required for leadership.

Practical Strategies for Setting and Maintaining Boundaries

If you've ever felt overwhelmed by endless requests and the pressure to be "always on," you're not alone. Many of us have been there. So let's dive into some practical strategies that can help you set—and, just as importantly, maintain—healthy boundaries without feeling like you're shutting people out.

1. Define Your Non-Negotiables

Start by stepping back and asking yourself: What is essential for my well-being and effectiveness? This could be as simple as carving out uninterrupted planning time each day, dedicating time for personal commitments, or even setting aside periods for a digital detox. Write these non-negotiables down. They are the core elements that allow you to show up fully in your professional and personal life.

For instance, maybe you need an hour in the morning when you have no interruptions—a time when you can set your intentions for the day. Or perhaps you recognize that a nightly wind-down routine is non-negotiable because it helps you recharge. Once you have identified these priorities, make them non-negotiable in your schedule.

2. Be Clear and Consistent

One of the most effective ways to maintain boundaries is to communicate them clearly and consistently. Let your team know if you decide you won't check emails after 7 p.m.. It might feel uncomfortable at first, but clarity breeds trust. When your expectations are transparent, everyone knows how to align with your schedule.

Consider creating a short message for your email signature or team communications that reinforces your boundaries. For example: "Please note: I do not check emails after 6 p.m. I will respond to your message the next business day." This simple step protects your time and models the importance of a healthy work-life balance for your team.

3. Delegate More

A common misconception is that leadership means doing everything yourself. In reality, effective leadership is about empowering others. When you delegate tasks, you conserve your energy and build capacity within your team. Look for opportunities to entrust responsibilities to your staff and provide them with the guidance they need to succeed. This not only lightens your load but also helps your team grow.

4. Schedule Boundaries into Your Calendar

Treat your personal time as an immovable appointment. Whether it's time for deep work, reflection, or simply downtime with your loved ones, block it out on your calendar. By scheduling these boundaries as you would a meeting, you signal to yourself and others that this time is sacred. Over time, you'll find that these protected blocks become the cornerstone of your productivity and well-being.

5. Learn to Say "No"

Perhaps the most challenging—but also the most empowering—strategy is learning to say "no." Many of us, especially in education, are naturally inclined to say "yes" because we want to help. However, constantly saying "yes" can lead to overcommitment and burnout. Remember: saying "no" is not a sign of weakness; it's a sign of self-respect and clear vision. Practice saying "no" in situations that would drain your energy, and notice how much more effective and centered you feel.

6. Set Priorities to Achieve Balance

Balance is really about boundaries, and that starts with setting clear priorities. Understanding what truly matters allows you to align your time and energy with your most important goals. Identify the tasks and commitments that best serve your well-being and focus on them. Once you've established these guiding priorities, everything else can fall into place, allowing you to stay centered and balanced in your life and work.

The Digital Dilemma: Managing Technology Boundaries

In today's world, technology is both a blessing and a curse. Our phones, laptops, and tablets keep us connected, but they can also blur the lines between work and personal life. The expectation of 24/7 availability is a recipe for exhaustion, and it can quickly erode the relational capacity that makes effective leadership possible.

Constant digital availability doesn't just drain time—it drains cognitive energy. Studies show that continuous digital distractions can impair our ability to concentrate on essential tasks, leading to decreased productivity, increased stress, and decision fatigue. The constant shifting of focus fragments our cognitive processes, making engaging in deep thinking and strategic leadership challenging. The more we allow digital demands to dictate our day, the less mental space we have for the deep thinking required for leadership. In other words, while technology can keep us connected, it can also leave us mentally fragmented and burned out (Rosen et al., 2011).

Setting Digital Limits

Ask yourself: Do you need to check your work email at midnight? If you wouldn't expect your team to respond during off-hours, why should you set a different standard for yourself? By setting clear digital boundaries, you protect your energy and model a healthier, more sustainable way of working.

Strategies to Manage Technology

- **Establish "Tech-Free" Times**: Designate specific hours in your day when you step away from your devices. This could be during family time in the evenings, during meals, or even a whole day each week if possible.
- **Use Auto-Responses**: If you're stepping away from your digital devices, consider setting up an automatic response on your email that indicates you will respond within a specific timeframe. This manages expectations and reduces the pressure to be instantly available.
- **Create Physical Boundaries**: Sometimes, it helps to disconnect physically. For example, consider keeping your work devices out of your bedroom or designating a space at home where work is not allowed.
- **Prioritize Notifications**: Review which notifications are essential and which can be silenced. Curating the constant stream of digital interruptions can help you reclaim more time and mental clarity.

Remember, setting digital boundaries is not about disconnecting entirely—it's about creating a rhythm that allows you to be fully present, whether at work or home.

Leadership Boundaries Across Different Audiences

Different audiences in our professional lives require different boundary-setting approaches. As a leader, you interact with staff, students, parents, and even district leaders; each group has its expectations. Tailoring your boundaries to each group makes you more effective and demonstrates consistency and fairness.

For Staff

Your staff looks to you for guidance, support, and direction. Being accessible is important, but so is modeling healthy boundaries. Encourage your team to try solving problems independently before coming to you, and be clear about your availability. When your staff sees you confidently managing your time, they learn that it's acceptable—and even necessary—to do the same.

Practical Tip: Hold regular meetings where you outline goals, expectations, and your availability. For example, let your team know you are available for drop-in consultations between 10 a.m. and noon and again in the late afternoon. You're dedicating time to deep work or personal recharge outside those hours.

For Students

Building strong relationships with students is at the heart of education. However, being approachable does not mean being available at all hours. Maintain clear professional boundaries while remaining supportive. When students see you balancing accessibility with self-care, they learn valuable lessons in managing their time and energy.

Practical Tip: Establish a routine that allows for both office hours and periods of focused work. Encourage students to come prepared with questions or issues during designated times, reinforcing that planning and respecting one's time are crucial skills.

For Parents

Parents often have high expectations for responsiveness and availability. Communicate when and how you can be reached to prevent last-minute stress and misunderstandings. Setting clear expectations with parents helps build a foundation of mutual respect and trust.

Practical Tip: Send out a brief communication at the start of the school year outlining your preferred methods and times for contact. For instance, specify that emails received after 6 p.m. will be addressed the following business day or that urgent matters should be communicated through a specific channel. This transparency helps manage expectations and prevents the feeling of constant urgency.

Tools for Setting and Maintaining Boundaries

Sometimes, even with the best intentions, our boundaries can become blurred. Fortunately, you can use practical tools and techniques to keep your limits firm and effective.

Conduct a Time Audit

Begin by taking a good, hard look at how you spend your day. A time audit isn't about self-criticism—it's about awareness. Track your activities for a week, noting where your time goes and where the "time drains" lie. This exercise can reveal patterns and help you identify opportunities for delegation or rescheduling.

How to Do It: Use a simple spreadsheet or a time-tracking app to log your daily activities. Review your log at the end of the week to see where you might be overcommitting. Perhaps you're spending too much time on emails or meetings that could be streamlined. Use this data to restructure your day to honor your non-negotiables.

Role-Play Boundary-Setting Scenarios

If you find it challenging to say "no" or articulate your boundaries, consider role-playing these scenarios with a trusted colleague. Practice common responses like, "I can't take this on right now, but let's figure out a way to make it work," or "I'm not available for a meeting at that time—can we reschedule?" With repeated practice, these conversations will become more natural and less stressful.

Practical Exercise: Set aside time with a colleague who understands your challenges. Role-play different scenarios and provide each other with feedback. This practice can build your confidence and help you refine your responses firmly and compassionately.

Set Clear Response-Time Expectations

Another helpful tool is to set clear expectations about response times. By letting your team know that you respond to emails within a specific timeframe—say, 24 hours—you relieve yourself from the pressure of immediate replies and teach everyone the value of measured communication.

Practical Tip: Include a note in your email signature or during team meetings that outlines your response policy. Over time, these expectations will become the norm, allowing for a more balanced workday.

Setting Boundaries at Home: The Leader's Toughest Challenge

While setting boundaries at work is challenging enough, establishing them at home can feel like an entirely different beast. Our professional responsibilities often spill over into our time, blurring the lines between our roles as leaders and as family members or individuals.

Protecting Your Personal Space

Your home is your sanctuary—a place to recharge, reflect, and be with loved ones. However, when work encroaches on personal time, you risk your well-being and the quality of your relationships. Protecting your personal time is not selfish; it's a necessary act of self-respect.

Practical Strategies:

- **Designate Tech-Free Zones**: Consider setting aside certain areas of your home, like your bedroom or the dining area, as work-free zones. This physical separation can help signal to yourself (and your family) that it's time to disconnect from work.
- **Establish a Digital Curfew**: Just as you might set a cut-off time for work emails, decide on an evening when you power down your devices. Whether it's 8 p.m. or 9 p.m., this digital curfew will allow you to transition from the workday to a period of rest and connection with those who matter most.
- **Schedule "Me-Time"**: Block out time in your calendar for activities that rejuvenate you—exercise, reading, or simply a quiet walk. When you treat these moments as sacred appointments, you reinforce the importance of personal well-being.

Navigating Family Expectations

It can be particularly challenging when family members are used to you being available at all hours. Clear communication is key. Explain your boundaries in a way that emphasizes your desire to be fully present when you are together.

Practical Tip: Have a family meeting where you share your work schedule and the boundaries you are setting. Explain that you can be the best version of yourself at work and at home by protecting your time.

Real-Life Stories: Lessons in Boundary Setting

Stories can be influential teachers. Over the years, I have encountered several real-life examples illustrating the transformative impact of setting healthy boundaries.

The Red Flyer Wagon Revisited

Let's revisit the story of the new teacher with the red flyer wagon. Each day, I saw her struggle under the weight of physical materials and unrealistic expectations. That simple act of stepping in, offering a hand, and reassuring her that "the world won't end" was a turning point. It wasn't just about alleviating the burden—it was a lesson in self-compassion and knowing one's limits. By modeling this behavior, I learned that leadership is as much about caring for yourself as it is about caring for others.

> Boundaries aren't about cutting people off; they're about saying "yes" to the things that matter most.

As a school leader, I thought I had seen it all. Budget cuts, policy changes, school safety concerns—every challenge had a solution, but nothing could have prepared me for the relentless pressure of leading a school during the COVID-19 pandemic. I had always prided myself on being available for my staff, students, and families, but suddenly, "available" became much more consuming.

With the transition to remote learning, my laptop became an extension of my body. I was glued to my screen from dawn until midnight, answering emails, attending virtual meetings, troubleshooting technology issues, and trying to ease the fears of my staff and school families. My phone vibrated constantly—parents worried about their children falling behind, teachers feeling overwhelmed by the demands of online instruction, and district leaders pushing out updates at all hours. It didn't matter if it was 6 AM or 11 PM—I felt obligated to respond immediately. At first, I convinced myself that this was temporary. "Just a few more weeks," I told myself, but as the weeks turned into months, my ability to separate work from home life evaporated entirely.

Physically, I was at home with my family. Mentally, I was somewhere else entirely. I missed meals, skipped workouts, and barely slept. I was running on fumes, and the worst part was that I didn't even understand how bad it had gotten until one evening, after I finished an hour-long conversation with a colleague, I realized I missed our family dinner. I wasn't just failing myself—I was failing my family.

One night, around midnight, I was lying on the couch, exhausted, staring blankly at my email inbox. It was never-ending. No matter how many messages I answered, more came flooding in. My body ached, my head throbbed, and a sinking realization settled over me: this wasn't sustainable. If I kept going at this pace, I would burn out completely—and I wasn't the only one. Teachers had confided in me that they, too, were struggling to balance their professional and personal lives. How could I expect them to if I didn't make a change?

That experience wasn't just a wake-up call for me—it was a leadership lesson I'll never forget. Sustainable leadership isn't about always being available; it's about being available at the correct times, with the right energy. If we don't model boundaries, our teams won't either. And if we don't protect our well-being, we can't expect those we lead to do the same.

A Commitment to Boundaries

When we finally returned to in-person learning, I knew I had to take action for myself and my entire staff. At our first faculty meeting back, I took a deep breath and addressed the elephant in the room. I shared my struggle with work-life balance, admitting how I had let the job demands consume me. I told them about the late nights, the constant pressure to be available, and the toll it had taken on my well-being and family. Then, I announced a new boundary: I would no longer answer emails outside duty days. If there was an emergency, staff members could call me directly; otherwise, emails and messages would wait until the next workday. At first, there was silence. Then, a few nods. And finally, a wave of visible relief.

Later that evening, my phone buzzed, but it wasn't a work crisis this time. Instead, I received several texts from staff members thanking me. One teacher wrote, *"I appreciate you setting this boundary. I didn't realize how much I needed permission to do the same."*

From that day forward, I made it my mission to maintain and model my boundaries for my staff. I stopped sending emails after school hours. Instead, I auto-scheduled my emails the next morning during the duty day. I encouraged my teachers to unplug after work hours and assured them that nothing short of an emergency needed immediate attention outside of school. Slowly, the culture of our school began to shift. Teachers felt less pressure to be "always on," and I could sense a renewed energy in our staff. It wasn't just about work-life balance—it was about well-being, about permitting ourselves to be present for the people who mattered most outside of school.

Remembering that we can't pour from an empty cup is essential. We are not serving our schools well if we are exhausted, distracted, and running on fumes. The best thing we can do for our students and staff is to model healthy boundaries and show them that taking care of ourselves and our families is not just okay—it's necessary. Setting boundaries isn't about neglecting responsibilities but creating a sustainable way to lead with empathy, energy, and effectiveness. And if we do it right, we won't just change our own lives—we'll change the culture of our schools for the better. So, take a step back. Close the laptop. Put down the phone. Be present for the people who love you. Your school will still be there in the morning, but these moments with your family? You can't get those back.

Final Thoughts: Leadership Sustainability Through Boundaries

As we close this chapter, let's take a moment to reflect on what we've explored. The best leaders aren't those who try to do everything—they are the ones who know what truly matters and have the courage to set boundaries that protect their energy and purpose.

Boundaries aren't about cutting people off; they're about saying "yes" to the things that matter most. By protecting your time and energy, you create space for deeper relationships, better decision-making, and a leadership journey that is both impactful and sustainable. Relational intelligence teaches us that self-awareness is key. When you honor your limits, you become a more effective leader and a model for those around you.

Remember: every time you say "no" to draining requests or unrealistic expectations, you're saying "yes" to sustainable leadership, quality connections, and the opportunity to make a difference. Boundaries aren't walls; they are the framework that allows us to build strong, sustainable connections that nurture trust, respect, and authenticity.

So, as you move forward, take a deep breath, trust your instincts, and remember that your well-being is the foundation upon which effective leadership is built. Embrace your non-negotiables, clearly communicate your limits, and honor the balance between work and life. Your journey as a leader will not only become more fulfilling—it will also inspire those around you to follow suit.

Thank you for taking the time to reflect on these ideas. May this chapter serve as both a guide and a reminder that the most powerful leadership comes from a place of balance, self-care, and genuine connection.

Best Practices in Action: Setting Boundaries with Purpose

As we wrap up this chapter, let's explore three best practices you can immediately apply to set boundaries, protect your well-being, and lead with more intention.

1. Implement "Power Hours" for Focused Work

One of the most effective ways to protect your time and energy is by carving out dedicated blocks of time during your day to focus solely on high-priority tasks—no distractions, no meetings, and no interruptions. Leaders set "Power Hours" to turn off their email, silence notifications, and dive into deep, uninterrupted work. It's a practice that's helped many of us avoid the constant tug-of-war between urgent tasks and meaningful work. By setting this boundary, you empower yourself to complete essential tasks with more clarity and purpose rather than reacting to every ping and request that comes your way.

2. Delegate with Confidence

Delegation isn't just about giving away tasks—it's about trusting your team to rise to the occasion. Leaders who set firm boundaries understand the importance of empowering others. If you're the one who is always taking on extra responsibilities, you're not allowing your staff to step up and grow. One simple but effective practice is to identify the tasks that others on your team can handle and give them the autonomy to take ownership. Doing this will lighten your load and foster a culture of trust and growth. When you confidently delegate, you show your team members that their contributions are valued.

3. Schedule Regular "No" Time

Sounds counterintuitive, right? But I promise you, one of the most effective strategies for leadership longevity is scheduling "no" time into your calendar. Whether it's an afternoon each week to recharge or a few hours set aside in the morning to reflect and reset, intentional "no" time is essential for sustaining your leadership energy. This time is for reconnecting with your personal goals, family, or self-care. When you protect these moments, you're reminding yourself and your team that your well-being matters, and in turn, you'll be a more present and effective leader.

By implementing these best practices, you're not just setting boundaries—you're fostering an environment where you and your team can thrive. Remember, leadership isn't about doing it all. It's about knowing what to prioritize, learning when to say no, and always keeping balance in mind. Ultimately, leaders who lead with energy and purpose, who set boundaries with intention, inspire the most significant transformation in those they serve.

CHAPTER TEN
Calm in the Chaos – Relational Intelligence in Crisis

Introduction

Crisis situations—whether an unforeseen school emergency, a pandemic, or a sudden change in leadership—are inevitable in any educational setting. These moments are filled with heightened emotions, uncertainty, and a palpable sense of disruption. However, what can truly make or break an educational leader during a crisis is not just their technical expertise but their ability to lead with **Relational Intelligence**.

In times of crisis, relationship-based leadership becomes the anchor that holds everything together. Relational Intelligence enables you to keep the team grounded, focused, and moving forward, despite the turbulence. Leaders who understand the power of relationships create a foundation of trust that can weather the storm and emerge stronger. This chapter dives deep into how relational intelligence plays a crucial role in navigating crises and how you can develop and refine your own RQ to be the calm in the storm.

> Relational Intelligence enables you to keep the team grounded, focused, and moving forward, despite the turbulence.

A few years ago, our school community faced a social media crisis. I remember it like it happened yesterday. The notifications came through my phone late one evening—dozens of messages, missed calls, and social media alerts began lighting up on my screen. At first, I thought it was just another routine school matter, but as I scrolled through the messages, my heart sank. A rumor had exploded on social media about a student medical incident that occurred earlier that week. The posts were filled with speculation, fear, and misinformation, quickly spiraling out of control.

The actual event had been severe but manageable. A student had suffered a seizure during lunch, and our staff had responded swiftly, calling 911, ensuring the student was safe, and following all emergency protocols. The student's parents were immediately contacted, and the student was receiving medical care. Still, when the story hit social media, the narrative had twisted into something far from reality. Rumors spread like wildfire. Some posts falsely claimed that the student had been unattended for too long. Others suggested that the school had mishandled the emergency, while a few exaggerated the severity of the student's condition. The speculation turned into anger within days, with parents demanding answers and community members sharing their frustration online. I knew that ignoring the situation wasn't an option. Trust is built on communication and honesty; the longer misinformation lingers, the harder it is to correct. I called an emergency staff meeting the following day before the students arrived.

Standing before my team, I acknowledged the tension in the room. Many of them had seen the online posts, and some were deeply upset by the misrepresentation of the situation. I reassured them that our response had been swift and by the book. I also reminded them that our first responsibility was to support each other and our students, not to get caught up in defending ourselves on social media. Together, we discussed what had happened and how we would move forward. Transparency was key. Our priority was making sure students felt informed in an age-appropriate way. Misinformation doesn't just stay on adult social media feeds—students hear things from their families, older siblings, or even each other. Teachers took moments in their classrooms that morning to acknowledge the incident. They shared basic, accurate information: that a student had a medical emergency, that staff had responded appropriately, and that the student was receiving care. They also reminded students about the importance of kindness, privacy, and avoiding speculation.

Still, I knew that the family concern wouldn't go away overnight. To address the broader community, I decided to host an in-person forum. I invited parents and caregivers to come and ask questions directly rather than relying on secondhand information online. Walking into the media center that night, I felt the moment's weight. Dozens of families were seated, some tense, others simply looking for reassurance. I opened the forum by stating my purpose: to listen, clarify, and move forward together. I shared the sequence of events, explaining the school's emergency protocols and how they had been followed. I acknowledged the fear that many parents felt when they first heard the rumors and empathized with their concerns. Then, I opened the floor for questions.

Some parents wanted reassurance that their children would be safe if they ever faced a medical emergency. Others were frustrated by the speed at which the misinformation had spread. One parent admitted to sharing a misleading post before knowing the whole story and regretted doing so. Through it all, I remained calm and focused on our shared goal—ensuring the safety and well-being of every student in our school. By the end of the evening, the tension in the room had eased. Parents thanked me for providing a space for open dialogue, and some even offered suggestions on improving communication in the future, such as a quicker messaging system for urgent updates. The meeting ended not with division but with a sense of understanding.

I watched the school community pull together over the next few weeks. Parents who had been vocal online started engaging more constructively—volunteering, attending school events, and even defending the school when misinformation popped up again. Teachers felt more confident in addressing concerns head-on rather than letting rumors fester. Even students seemed to internalize the lesson, becoming more thoughtful about how quickly false information can spread. In the end, the crisis became an opportunity for growth. The experience reinforced an important lesson for me as a school leader: trust isn't just given—it's earned, nurtured, and, when necessary, rebuilt. In moments of crisis, people don't just need policies and procedures—they need honesty, empathy, and a leader willing to stand before them, listen, and lead with integrity. This experience reinforced a crucial truth: during a crisis, technical responses alone are not enough—what truly stabilizes a school is relational intelligence. When leaders approach crises with trust, transparency, and emotional awareness, they turn moments of disruption into opportunities for unity and growth.

The Importance of Relationship-Based Leadership During Crises

When a crisis strikes, the instinct is often to jump into action—implementing new protocols, communicating with external stakeholders, or solving immediate problems. While these actions are necessary, they should be grounded in a foundation of relationships. A crisis tests a team's cohesion, and relationship-based leadership is key to maintaining stability in such uncertain times.

Relationship-driven leadership fosters trust, empathy, and understanding, precisely what is needed when emotions run high. Here's why relational leadership is critical in times of crisis:

- **Trust Acts as the Bedrock**: Trust is your currency in a crisis. Without trust in each other and the leadership, chaos can quickly spread. Leaders who model transparency, vulnerability, and empathy can keep teams united and focused on solutions.
- **Emotional Resilience**: Leading with relational intelligence ensures team members have a safe space to express their concerns and emotions. Emotional resilience, both for leaders and teams, becomes stronger when there is an open channel for communication and when individuals feel supported.

- **Crisis is a Team Effort**: Crisis management requires collaboration. A relational leader doesn't work alone—they empower their team, encourage input from all stakeholders, and rely on team-based problem-solving to overcome challenges together.

Techniques for Managing Emotional Contagion, Transparent Communication, and Team-Based Problem Solving

In the middle of a crisis, emotions can spread like wildfire. Anxiety, fear, and frustration can be contagious, and leaders need to manage emotional contagion while ensuring that the team remains productive and engaged. Here are some essential techniques for managing emotions, maintaining transparency, and facilitating collaborative problem-solving:

1. **Emotional Contagion Management**:
   - **Model Calmness**: As a leader, your emotional state can directly affect the mood of your team. You set the tone for others by modeling a calm and steady demeanor. While you must acknowledge the gravity of the situation, you must maintain composure and optimism.
   - **Practice Active Listening**: Let your team express their concerns and emotions without judgment. When people feel heard, they are less likely to let anxiety or frustration take over.
   - **Normalize Feelings**: In a crisis, emotions run high. Acknowledge the collective feelings of uncertainty and stress. Validate those feelings, but also reframe the situation to focus on solutions. This helps people move from emotional reaction to thoughtful action.

2. **Transparent Communication**:
   - **Be Open and Honest**: Misinformation or silence can breed distrust and panic during a crisis. Leaders must remain open and transparent about what is known and unknown. Let your team know the current situation and its evolution, even if it is still uncertain.
   - **Clarify Expectations and Roles**: When things are chaotic, confusion around roles and responsibilities can add more stress. Communicate clearly about each person's role and how they can contribute to the crisis response.
   - **Frequent Updates**: Regular, clear updates keep the team in-

formed and help minimize uncertainty. This builds a sense of control in an environment that may feel uncontrollable.

3. **Team-Based Problem Solving**:
    - **Collaborative Decision-Making**: In a crisis, every voice counts. Invite your team to brainstorm solutions together. Don't just dictate the course of action—empower your team to contribute their perspectives and insights.
    - **Divide and Conquer**: Break down the problem into smaller, manageable pieces and assign tasks to different team members based on their strengths. This makes the crisis more manageable and allows people to take ownership of their contributions.
    - **Flexibility and Adaptability**: In crises, the landscape is constantly changing. Leaders must encourage an agile mindset, where problem-solving isn't rigid but adaptable to the evolving situation. Create a culture where it's okay to pivot when necessary.

Real-World Examples: Relational Intelligence in Action During Crisis

The COVID-19 Pandemic: During the COVID-19 pandemic, many school leaders faced unprecedented challenges. Mrs. Jenkins, a high school district principal hit hard by the crisis, demonstrated exceptional relational intelligence. She initiated weekly virtual check-ins with her teachers to discuss curriculum and prioritize their mental health and emotional well-being. She fostered a trusting environment that reduced burnout and encouraged collaboration during uncertain times by openly sharing information, acknowledging challenges, and ensuring access to support.

Natural Disaster Response: In the aftermath of Hurricane Katrina, school leaders had to navigate an enormous crisis. Mr. Edwards, a principal in New Orleans, relied on his strong relationships with staff and the community to build an emergency response plan. His emphasis on open communication and involving teachers in decision-making empowered the team to act cohesively, stay focused, and rebuild the school quickly. The relational trust he cultivated during the crisis played a crucial role in their recovery and long-term resilience.

Managing a School Lockdown: A school was put into lockdown in a small district due to a nearby threat. Principal Davis focused on maintaining calm and clear communication throughout the ordeal. He kept staff informed of the situation and checked in with them regularly to ensure they felt supported and equipped to handle the anxiety among students. After the lockdown ended, he held debriefing sessions to address emotional challenges and to discuss strategies for better crisis preparedness. His transparency and concern for his team's well-being helped foster a sense of unity and trust that carried the school through future crises.

Wildfire Evacuation: A principal in a rural district had to lead his school through an evacuation when nearby wildfires threatened the area. He relied on strong relationships with local authorities, parents, and teachers to ensure the safe evacuation of students. Throughout the evacuation process, he maintained a calm, decisive presence and communicated frequently with staff, ensuring they knew their roles and felt supported. His relational intelligence allowed the staff to act swiftly and effectively, demonstrating that trust and open communication are key to managing crises.

These examples highlight the power of relational intelligence in crisis leadership. Whether navigating a global pandemic, natural disasters, or local emergencies, leaders who prioritize transparent communication, emotional support, and collaboration help create resilient teams. By fostering trust and empowering staff, school leaders can ensure their teams remain focused, supported, and capable of overcoming any challenge that comes their way.

Crisis Protocol Exercises to Build Resilience

Building relational intelligence requires preparation, practice, and reflection. Below are some exercises to strengthen relational leadership in crises:

1. **Scenario Planning and Role-playing**: Create realistic crisis scenarios (e.g., natural disaster, school lockdown, or public relations issue) and role-play these situations with your team. Focus on communication, emotional management, and collaboration during these exercises. The goal is to practice staying calm, communicating clearly, and working as a team in a high-pressure environment.
2. **Post-Crisis Debriefing**: After any crisis—big or small—hold a debriefing meeting where you and your team reflect on what went well, what didn't, and how to improve for next time. Discuss the emotional toll of the crisis and how team members supported one another. These debriefs can strengthen your relational bonds and increase resilience for future challenges.
3. **Building Trust through Small Wins**: Practice relational leadership in low-stakes situations to build trust. Take the time to have one-on-

one conversations with your team, celebrate small wins, and demonstrate that you value their contributions. These practices make the trust needed to weather a more significant crisis later.

Conclusion

In crises, leadership is tested not only by decisions and actions but by the ability to maintain calm and trust within the team. **Relational Intelligence** offers a roadmap for navigating uncertainty with empathy, communication, and collaboration. You can confidently lead through any crisis by fostering strong relationships, practicing transparent communication, and encouraging team-based problem-solving. Ultimately, your ability to stay calm, grounded, and connected to your team will define your success as a leader during chaotic times.

By making relational intelligence a cornerstone of your leadership approach, you build resilience within your team, ensuring that even in the most challenging moments, everyone stays united, focused, and ready to emerge stronger on the other side.

There are moments when a leader's presence profoundly impacts you—moments that stay with you long after the event itself—one of those moments happened on my very first day of high school. I had just moved to a new school, and amid the whirlwind of adjustments, I received heartbreaking news: my grandfather had passed away. My parents had to check me out of school about an hour before the end of the day. But as we walked toward the parking lot, something unexpected happened that I've never forgotten.

Mr. Kent, our high school principal, walked out to meet us in the parking lot. He stopped, looked me in the eye, and offered genuine condolences. "I'm so sorry for your loss," he said, his tone filled with empathy. And then, in a moment that spoke volumes about his leadership, he told my parents and me, "Don't worry about school work. You have the whole year ahead. Don't give this another thought until you get back." It was a simple statement, but conveyed so much more to me. He wasn't just doing his job as a principal; he was showing up as a leader who understood that relationships—human connection—were far more critical than any assignment or academic deadline.

That moment with Mr. Kent was a powerful reminder that **leadership is not just about being present in body but fully present in every moment**. His words, genuine compassion, and focused attention on my needs in a time of loss set him apart as a leader. He didn't just show up; he was there with his heart, full attention, and unwavering commitment to the people he led.

This concept of being "fully present" is the foundation of meaningful leadership. While many leaders may show up to meetings and events, it's not always the case that they are genuinely *engaged*. I realized this over the years: being physically present is only part of the equation. The true power lies in being emotionally and mentally involved in every interaction, big or small. It's about offering your undivided attention and, in doing so, making others feel genuinely seen and heard.

The Difference Between Being Present and Being Fully Present

We've all experienced meetings in which our bodies are in the room but our minds are elsewhere—distracted by emails, lost in thought, or mentally moving on to the next task. This is the difference between merely being present and truly being fully present.

Being present means showing up physically, but being fully present requires something much deeper. It means aligning your mind, body, and emotions with the moment, offering your full attention to the people and the task. Engaging fully makes your interactions richer, more impactful, and meaningful. These moments are the cornerstone for building trust, strengthening relationships, and cultivating a leadership presence that leaves a lasting, transformative impact.

> Being present means showing up physically, but being fully present requires something much deeper.

The Power of Presence: A Leader's Lesson

Early in my career as a school leader, I prided myself on being accessible. My email inbox was a never-ending stream of questions, concerns, and urgent requests, and I had convinced myself that responding quickly was a sign of strong leadership. Whether in my office, the hallways, or a team meeting, I kept an eye on my messages in case something needed my immediate attention. I thought I was being efficient. I didn't realize that I was unintentionally sending the message that the people right in front of me weren't my priority in my attempt to be responsive to all.

That realization hit me unexpectedly one afternoon when a department leader stopped by my office. He started by thanking me for my commitment to supporting teachers and for always being available when they needed me. I smiled, thinking it was just a casual moment of appreciation. But then he shifted in his chair and said, "I wanted to share something with you—something I think might help our meetings feel more productive." I leaned in, curious. "I've noticed that you often check your email during team data meetings. I completely understand that you have a lot on your plate, and I respect how available you are to everyone. But sometimes, when we're having important discussions, it feels like we don't have your full attention." I blinked, caught off guard. I opened my mouth to explain—indeed, I could multitask. I had always been able to skim an email while still listening to the conversation. But then, I saw the sincerity in his expression, and I stopped myself. This wasn't a complaint but an honest attempt to help me see something I had been blind to.

He continued, "Our conversations in those meetings are crucial. And I know you care. It would mean a lot to the team if you could be fully present in those moments." I thanked him for his honesty and assured him I'd reflect on what they said. Later that evening, I sat at my desk, replaying the conversation. At first, I wanted to justify my actions. I wasn't ignoring my staff but trying to balance it all. But the more I thought about it, the more I realized he was right. I had always expected teachers to fully engage in their classrooms and give their students their undivided attention. But what kind of example was I setting if I couldn't even give my teachers the same courtesy? How could I expect my staff to value collaboration if I was distracted during some of our most crucial discussions?

The following day, I made a decision. I addressed the room at the start of our next team data meeting. I acknowledged my habit of checking emails during meetings and admitted that, while I had intended to stay on top of things, I now realized it was coming at the cost of being fully present with them. I committed right then and there: going forward, I would put my phone and laptop away during meetings. No emails, no distractions. Just listening, learning, and engaging in the conversations that mattered. The response was immediate. Some teachers nodded in appreciation. Others looked genuinely surprised that I had acknowledged it so openly. After the meeting, several staff members approached me privately to say they respected my willingness to make a change.

Over the next few weeks, I noticed a shift in myself and the team. Our meetings felt more collaborative. Conversations flowed more easily. I was picking up on details I had likely missed before. Teachers were more open, more engaged, and, in turn, I found myself learning from them in ways I hadn't before. One teacher even joked, "I was waiting for you to glance at your email at least once today—but you didn't! It means a lot." That moment reaffirmed what I had learned: Presence matters. Leadership isn't just about being available to everyone all the time—it's about being fully present for the people in front of you.

From that day on, I became more intentional about when and where I checked my emails. Emergencies would still find their way to me if necessary, but for everything else? It could wait. My time with my staff was valuable, and I needed to model that belief in my actions, not just my words. I share this experience with other school leaders now because I know how easy it is to fall into the trap of constant connectivity. But if we want people to feel valued, we must show them they have our full attention. That their time, their ideas, and their voices matter. And sometimes, the best way to lead is by simply putting the phone away and listening.

The Reality of Distractions in Leadership

In today's fast-paced world, distractions are inevitable. Research tells us that we're only fully engaged about 50% of the time. The rest of the time, our attention is split between checking emails, responding to texts, thinking ahead to the next meeting, or mentally juggling our many responsibilities. Though often seen as necessary, multitasking distracts us from fully engaging in the moment. Switching between tasks depletes our cognitive resources and reduces our ability to concentrate on any one thing.

Research indicates that it takes, on average, 23 minutes to regain focus after an interruption (Mark, Gonzalez, & Harris, 2005). For school leaders, this means you lose critical moments for connection with your staff and students each time you're distracted, whether by a phone call or your to-do list. These lost moments can accumulate quickly, impairing your ability to make informed decisions, solve problems, and, most importantly, build trust with your team.

Too often, we think we can juggle multiple things at once, but the truth is that multitasking makes us less effective. When you're divided between answering emails, thinking about tomorrow's meeting, or running through your mental checklist, you're not fully present for those you lead. Without full attention, relationships falter. If you're not fully listening or your body language isn't conveying your interest and engagement, the message sent is a disconnection, even if that's not your intention.

It's essential to realize that while multitasking might seem like an efficient way to handle leadership demands, it often comes at the cost of quality engagement. Over time, this erodes relationships, diminishes trust, and leads to more significant stress and burnout.

Mindful Leadership Practices for Being Fully Present

To lead effectively, we need to be mindful. Mindful leadership doesn't simply mean showing up physically; it means showing up with your heart, mind, and presence. Mindfulness involves being intentional, being present with the people and tasks before you, and consciously focusing on the now. This mindset can radically shift how we show up as leaders, ensuring our focus remains on the relationships that matter most.

Here are some mindful leadership practices that can help you become fully present in your leadership role:

1. Active Listening

Authentic listening is more than just hearing words. It requires us to focus on the speaker, understanding their emotions and intentions behind what's being said. Active listening includes asking open-ended questions and providing feedback that shows engagement. When teachers or staff members come to you with concerns or ideas, give them your full attention. Put away your phone, turn off your laptop, and listen—really listen. Let them know that their voice matters.

2. Set Boundaries for Undivided Attention

As a school leader, it is easy to get pulled in multiple directions. However, when someone comes to you, give them your full attention. This may mean setting boundaries around your time and energy and scheduling regular moments for undistracted conversations. Teach your staff that you value their time by setting an example and prioritizing focused attention.

3. Non-Verbal Cues

Your body language speaks volumes. When engaging with staff, make sure your posture conveys openness and attentiveness. Nodding, making eye contact, and using open gestures indicate your presence. These non-verbal cues can distinguish between a genuine connection and a disjointed conversation.

4. Pause and Reflect

In the rush of school leadership, glossing over the quieter moments is easy. But pausing to reflect—whether after a conversation or a decision—allows you to assess your engagement level and recalibrate. If your attention drifts, take a step back, breathe, and ground yourself in the present moment. Reflection helps you reset and be more mindful in your interactions moving forward.

The Impact of Being Fully Present on School Culture

When you are fully present as a leader, the impact extends beyond the immediate conversation. Being fully present builds stronger relationships with your staff, fosters a culture of trust, and creates a sense of community. Teachers who feel seen and heard are likelier to be engaged, motivated, and willing to invest in the school's mission. Your leadership becomes a model for others, showing them the value of engagement and presence.

It's no secret that school culture is rooted in the quality of relationships. When relationships are strong, the school environment becomes one where collaboration thrives, communication flows freely, and everyone feels like a valued part of the team. This is the essence of relational leadership. Your ability to be present helps shape the environment in which your staff and students can flourish.

When teachers feel connected to you as a leader, they're more likely to stay, especially in times of difficulty. A genuinely supported and heard teacher is more likely to remain in their role, contributing positively to the school's culture. Conversely, a distracted or disengaged leader can foster a sense of disconnect and dissatisfaction, leading to high turnover and disengagement.

How Being Fully Present Can Transform Your Leadership

The benefits of being fully present as a leader go beyond improved relationships—they directly influence the effectiveness of your decision-making. When present, you're more likely to absorb critical information, ask insightful questions, and offer well-informed guidance. Decisions made while fully engaged are often more thoughtful and attuned to the needs of your team.

Additionally, being present in moments of crisis or challenge allows you to lead with clarity and calm. During difficult times, your ability to stay grounded, listen, and respond thoughtfully can provide the stability your school community needs. Your presence reassures staff and students that you're in control, committed, and there for them.

A study from Harvard Business Review found that employees who feel heard by their leaders are 4.6 times more likely to feel empowered to perform their best work. This underscores the power of listening, of being fully present—physically, emotionally, and mentally. When you listen deeply, you open the door to new possibilities and solutions. You strengthen relationships, enhance problem-solving, and create a more inclusive and empowering environment.

The Role of Presence in Managing Crisis

In times of crisis, your ability to remain calm and present can significantly impact the outcomes. Whether navigating a school-wide issue, a student's emotional crisis, or a leadership challenge, your level of engagement can amplify or alleviate the tension. Leaders who are scattered or distracted in times of crisis may inadvertently exacerbate the situation. On the other hand, a present leader, both emotionally and mentally, can provide the clarity and support their team needs to navigate the challenge effectively.

Being present also allows you to make decisions with greater empathy and understanding. When you're fully engaged with the situation at hand, you're more likely to understand the needs of those affected, create solutions that address those needs, and communicate in a way that reassures and empowers.

Conclusion: Relational Intelligence — The Key to Effective Leadership

As we close, remember this: Relational Intelligence is the cornerstone of effective leadership. Leadership is about people—building connections that empower, support, and appreciate those we lead. The most impactful leaders know their success lies in their ability to connect, communicate, and care for others.

At the heart of relational intelligence is being fully present in every moment with every individual. Small, everyday actions—the hallway chats, the check-ins, the smile after a tough meeting—make people feel seen, heard, and valued. These moments often shape someone's sense of belonging and commitment.

> The most impactful leaders know their success lies in their ability to connect, communicate, and care for others.

We often think grand gestures matter, but the truth is that everyday presence fuels trust, respect, and inspiration. Truly engaged leaders inspire their teams to show up fully and bring their best selves to the work.

So, as you move forward, remember: Relational Intelligence is your most powerful tool. The relationships you nurture through presence and care create dynamic, successful teams. In a world full of distractions, the gift of your full attention is one of the most powerful ways to lead. Lead with presence, and watch the impact unfold.

As I think back to my principal's actions from 40 years ago, I realize the impact they still have today. Will your actions resonate like that? Will people mention you in a book years from now, with a smile, because of the way you led? It won't be because you were the most intelligent or dynamic person in the room. It will be because of the relationships you built and the genuine focus you gave to others.

Leadership Challenge: Over the next week, commit to one small act of relational leadership:

- Practice full presence. Put away your phone during key meetings and give your full attention.
- Have a five-minute "hallway check-in" with a staff member—just to listen, not to solve.
- Publicly acknowledge a teacher's unique strength and how it's making a difference.

These small shifts will transform your leadership, deepen trust, and create a culture where every team member feels valued. Leadership isn't about being perfect—it's about showing up, again and again, for the people who need you.

Ultimately, I hope you never forget my favorite quote: *"Effective leadership is leaving people better than you found them!"* That, my friends, is the power of Relational Intelligence.

REFERENCES

Avolio, B. J., & Gardner, W. L. (2005). Authentic leadership development: Getting to the root of positive forms of leadership. *The Leadership Quarterly, 16*(3), 315–338.

Baumeister, R. F., Bratslavsky, E., Finkenauer, C., & Vohs, K. D. (2001). Bad is stronger than good. *Review of General Psychology, 5*(4), 323–370.

Boyatzis, R. E. (2018). *The competent manager: A model for effective performance.* Wiley.

Boyatzis, R. E., & McKee, A. (2005). *Resonant leadership: Renewing yourself and connecting with others through mindfulness, hope, and compassion.* Harvard Business Press.

Brown, B. (2018). *Dare to lead: Brave work. Tough conversations. Whole hearts.* Random House.

Bryk, A. S., & Schneider, B. (2002). *Trust in schools: A core resource for improvement.* Russell Sage Foundation.

Caldwell, C., & Hayes, L. A. (2016). Leadership and trust: Their impact on the organizational culture. *Journal of Leadership & Organizational Studies, 23*(4), 371–387. https://doi.org/10.1177/1548051816642320

Cameron, K. S., & Quinn, R. E. (2011). *Diagnosing and changing organizational culture: Based on the competing values framework.* Pearson Education.

Center for American Progress. (2015). *The case for teacher leadership: Creating a sustainable career path for teachers.* https://cdn.americanprogress.org/wp-content/uploads/2015/07/TeacherLeadership-report.pdf

Cherniss, C. (2010). Emotional intelligence: Toward clarification of a concept. *Industrial and Organizational Psychology, 3*(2), 110–126. https://doi.org/10.1111/j.1754-9434.2010.01231.x

Cloud, H., & Townsend, J. (2017). *Boundaries: When to say yes, how to say no to take control of your life*. Zondervan.

Covey, S. R. (2006). *The speed of trust: The one thing that changes everything*. Free Press.

Crawford, C. B., Kuntz, L. A., & Stoker, G. R. (2019). The power of authentic leadership: Enhancing organizational performance through integrity and emotional intelligence. *Journal of Leadership Studies, 13*(4), 27–42. https://doi.org/10.1002/jls.21657

Darling-Hammond, L., Hyler, M. E., & Gardner, M. (2017). *Effective teacher professional development*. Learning Policy Institute. https://learningpolicyinstitute.org/product/effective-teacher-professional-development-report

Edmondson, A. C. (2019). *The fearless organization: Creating psychological safety in the workplace for learning, innovation, and growth*. Wiley.

Fullan, M. (2001). *Leading in a culture of change*. Jossey-Bass.

Gallup, Inc. (2017). *State of the American workplace: Employee engagement insights for U.S. business leaders*. Gallup Press. https://www.gallup.com/workplace/257578/state-american-workplace-report-2017.aspx

Gallup. (2020). *State of the global workplace: Employee engagement insights for business leaders worldwide*. Gallup, Inc. https://www.gallup.com/workplace/349484/state-of-the-global-workplace.aspx

Goleman, D. (2013). *Emotional intelligence: Why it can matter more than IQ*. Bantam.

Gordon, J. (2007). *The energy bus: 10 rules to fuel your life, work, and team with positive energy*. Wiley.

Gottman, J., & Levenson, R. (n.d.). The magic relationship ratio, according to science. *The Gottman Institute*. https://www.gottman.com/blog/the-magic-relationship-ratio-according-science/

Granovetter, M. S. (1973). The strength of weak ties. *American Journal of Sociology, 78*(6), 1360–1380. https://doi.org/10.1086/225469

Hanover Research. (2020). *Action guide: Characteristics of high-performing schools*. Hanover Research.

Hanover Research. (2020). *Teacher leadership in high-performing schools*. Hanover Research.

Hargreaves, A. (2000). Mixed emotions: Teachers' perceptions of their interactions with students. *Teaching and Teacher Education, 16*(8), 811–826. https://doi.org/10.1016/S0742-051X(00)00043-2

Hargreaves, A., & Fullan, M. (2012). *Professional capital: Transforming teaching in every school.* Teachers College Press.

Hattie, J. (2009). *Visible learning: A synthesis of over 800 meta-analyses relating to achievement.* Routledge.

AUTHOR BIO
Dr. Brad Johnson

Dr. Brad Johnson is a globally recognized educational leader, speaker, and author with over 30 years of experience transforming schools. Dr. Johnson is ranked #3 among the top 30 Global Gurus in Education and is passionate about empowering educators to maximize their potential through strong relationships, communication, and collaboration.

Author of 15 influential books, including *Empowering Students, Finding Your Leadership Edge, Becoming a More Assertive Teacher,* and the bestseller *Dear Teacher*, Dr. Johnson offers practical guidance for educators at all levels. His work is rooted in relational intelligence and servant leadership, helping school leaders build authentic, trust-based connections with their teams.

Dr. Johnson, a highly sought-after speaker, has presented in 10 countries and hosts the *Lattes with Leaders* podcast. He inspires educators worldwide

with his message of leadership rooted in empathy and effective communication. His work demonstrates the transformative power of leadership that prioritizes people, creating lasting positive change in schools and communities. For speaking availability or more information about Dr. Johnson's work, visit www.DoctorBradJohnson.com

Want to read more from Brad? Grab your copy of *Empowering Students* at www.teacher-goals.com/empower

AUTHOR BIO
Dr. Rachel Edoho-Eket

Dr. Rachel Edoho-Eket is a wife, mother, principal, author, speaker, and the 2025 President of the Maryland Association of Elementary School Principals. With decades as a teacher and leader in public education, she has earned a reputation as a strong instructional leader, passionate educational advocate, and dedicated mentor. As the Principal of a National Blue Ribbon school in Maryland, she is a lifelong learner who strives for excellence for herself and everyone she serves. She also serves as an adjunct professor at McDaniel College, helping to support the personal and professional growth of aspiring and current school leaders.

Dr. Edoho-Eket's belief in fostering meaningful relationships serves as the foundation for everything she does, and her highly effective teaching and leadership style continue to inspire up-and-coming aspiring teacher leaders.

During her educational career, she has proudly served as a classroom teacher, instructional team leader, mentor teacher, Assistant Principal, and Principal. Her first best-selling book, "The Principal's Journey: Navigating the Path to School Leadership," provides a helpful and practical blueprint for educators to follow as they transition into new leadership roles. Dr. Edoho-Eket holds a B.S. in Early Childhood and Elementary Education from Temple University, an M.S. in Curriculum and Instruction from McDaniel College, and a Doctorate in Leadership and Professional Practice from Trevecca Nazarene University.

To invite Dr. Edoho-Eket to speak at your next event, please visit www.racheledohoeket.com.